# Looking
# for
# Home

# Looking
# for
# Home

## Women Writing about Exile

Edited by Deborah Keenan and Roseann Lloyd

MILKWEED EDITIONS

**Looking for Home**

©Milkweed Editions 1990
All rights reserved
Printed in the United States of America
Post Office Box 3226
Minneapolis, MN 55403
Books may be ordered from the above address

93 92 91 90    4 3 2 1

ISBN: 0-915943-45-X

Publication of this book is made possible in part by grant support from the Literature Program of the National Endowment for the Arts, the Arts Development Fund of United Arts, the Dayton Hudson Foundation for Dayton's and Target Stores, the First Bank Systems Foundation, the General Mills Foundation, Jerome Foundation, the Star-Tribune/Cowles Media Company, the Minnesota State Arts Board through an appropriation by the Minnesota State Legislature, a McKnight Foundation Award administered by the Minnesota State Arts Board, the Northwest Area Foundation, and the support of generous individuals.

808.81
LOO

Library of Congress Cataloging-in-Publication Data

Looking for home: women writing about exile
edited by Roseann Lloyd and Deborah Keenan

p. cm.
ISBN 0-915943-45-X; $11.95
1. Poetry—Women authors. 2. Poetry, Modern—20th century.
3. Literature—Exiled authors. 4. Exiles—Poetry. 5. Authors, Exiled—Poetry.
6. Alienation (Social psychology)—Poetry.
I. Lloyd, Roseann. II. Keenan, Deborah.
PN6109.9.L66 1990
808.81 0082—dc20                                      89-13563
                                                         CIP

♾

The paper used in this publication meets the minimum requirements of American National Standard for Information Services — Permanence of Paper for Printed Library Materials, ANSI Z39.48-1984.

This book is dedicated
to all the women
whose stories have been lost.

# Preface

Over the last few years, we have read many wonderful poems written by American women who were born in other countries and spoke other languages as children. These women have gone through many culture shocks in one lifetime: war, relocation, immigration, a change in languages; they are now writing in English as naturally as others born to American English.

Fluent in American English, some of the writers use words from their other language/s in their poems. We became fascinated with the idea of bilingual poems, a text that plays with languages, as in work such as "A Black Night in Haiti, Palais National, Port-au-Prince," by Ntozake Shange. In this poem Shange uses both Spanish and French in the English text and this mix conveys the criss-crossing cultures that make the story of this hemisphere.

We wondered if other women were playing with language in this way. We thought that if we in the Midwest knew women born halfway around the globe, then surely there were many more women across the country who were writing the stories of their lives. Of course we knew of fiction writers, such as Lore Segal and Bharati Mukherjee, but we wanted to find the poets.

And so the idea for the book was born. We thank Emilie Buchwald, the co-publisher of Milkweed Editions, for immediately encouraging us.

We sent out a call for submissions and received thousands of poems in response. We wanted poems grounded in American English, poems by women who are living here, intending to stay here. We wanted bilingual poems. We didn't ask for translations because there are already publications of translated poems (although in the end some translations were included in the book).

We received over 2,000 poems in a wide range of forms: narrative poems, lyric poems, prose poems, chants, visual poetry, new forms we hadn't yet imagined. We received poems showing many viewpoints and perspectives on the idea of exile: chosen exile, forced exile, immigration, emigration, as well as the idea of exile within the dominant culture—poems by women who see themselves as living in exile within the dominant white-male culture. Exile as metaphor brings to life the reality of the economic exile of divorce, the isolation brought on by domestic abuse, chemical dependency, and child abuse. The metaphor brings to life the loss of connection that many women have experienced in this culture. The word *exile* suggests political connotations, and spiritual overtones; it suggests a search in the wilderness for meaning, now in 1989, fifty years after the start of World War II, the major disruption of our time. We also received poems that reflect on the word *home*, poems that create the connections that give us a home in spite of disconnections. The tension between the words *home* and *exile* gives a continuum—the poems place themselves anywhere between rootedness and restlessness.

As we worked through the poems that came in the mail, other poems came to mind, old favorites which we love in a new way in the context of this book so we solicited some of these poems, such as "Epiphany," by Nancy Paddock.

The poems came from all over the United States, from San Diego to New York City, from Miami to Seattle, from Putney, Vermont to Castro Valley, California, from Pittsburgh, Pennsylvania to Stafford, Texas. The language backgrounds were as diverse as the locations: Spanish, Chinese, Japanese, Tagalog, Illocono, Hindi, Hungarian, Latvian, German, and others. We found it impressive that many of the women are writing in English as their third or fourth language. Ilze Mueller, for example, was born in Latvia and spoke Latvian until the end of World War II. Then she was in a refugee camp in Germany and spoke German. She attended a French school and learned French at this time. Her family emigrated to Australia where she learned her fourth language, English. Later, Ilze lived in Chicago, New York, and St. Paul. She lived for some time in the country which was then known as the Belgian Congo, now Zaire. Dina Uahupirapi's original language is Herero. In order to go to school in Namibia, she had to learn Afrikaans. Now she is studying in St. Paul and learning English as her third language.

———

All the submitted poems reflected amazing life histories. Our interest in how women live made our reading slow. We lived with the poems for a long time, letting them sink into our consciousness. In the end, we selected poems that stayed with us, with thoughts and images that haunted us, the ones that were esthetically finished and powerful in their meaning.

We wanted to include strong poems from as many cultures as possible. We assumed that there would not be "unity" among various cultural groups. As Shirley Geok-Lin Lim writes in the introduction to the fine anthology *The Forbidden Stitch: An Asian American Women's Anthology*:

> If the women's movement has discovered "difference" to be a liberating rather than oppressive principle, through which new visions, new understandings, and new orders of society can be generated, the experience of being an "Asian American woman" is an exemplar of living in difference. Despite the still-flourishing stereotype of the "Asian American woman" as more submissive, more domestic, and therefore, in a dominantly patriarchal society, more sexually available than her other American sisters, Asian American women exhibit a bewildering display of differences. We do not share a common history, a common original culture or language, not even a common physique or color. . . .

This view of differences holds for all the women whose poems are included in this anthology, those who might be labelled "Hispanic," or "European." Each woman speaks both out of her culture and for herself.

Yet while we acknowledge differences, we also see similarities. We saw some common themes emerging from 2,000+ poems: concern for the "divided heart," respect for traditions, living in two cultures at once, a concern about domestic abuse and militarism, the strong drive to find a language that represents our experience as women.

We were especially gratified to discover many bilingual poems, from many languages. We discovered Irena Klepfisz's essay about writing:

———

I want to contribute towards a literature which is rooted in my experience, which reflects the special place Yiddish has had in my life. So I have been experimenting to see if I could reflect in my writing the two linguistic and cultural worlds to which I am committed. So far I have only finished two poems in which Yiddish plays a major part. . . . Neither quite escapes from intellectual formulation into the active imaginative expression of poetic form. This can only happen with repeated experimentation and feeling more *heymish*, comfortable, with the idea. I need time and patience.

We have included one of the poems she refers to. With all due respect to the writer, in our opinion the poem does make the leap into poetry, as do the other bilingual poems we have included. The bilingual poems bring an intensity and a global vision to the act of writing. Meredith Stricker, one of the contributors, writes:

My mother tongue is English, but my mother's tongue (*anya nylv*) is Hungarian—taken from her by World War II. I have always felt this separation from a mother tongue while leaning toward what I can hardly name—a true voice freely exchanged that the poems want to speak—a first language. What emerges from this longing: a dislocation from, distrust of the given official language. A sense of loss: that every English word my mother taught me dissolved one of her own. . . . Dissolution of one's own language became for me a parable of atomic threat. That not just the individual voice—but all voice may perish. My mother's name—Eva—fused in the poems with the story of Eurydice: women sent far from their borders, not allowed return. Eurydice irradiated—turned to "smoke in all directions" by Orpheus' gaze, the borderguard's searchlight. So I keep leaning toward a poetry that recognizes and refuses the possibility of such radical dispersal, making of exile a bridge.

Not long ago, I dreamed of traveling by car in a large, underground cave. A woman embraced me and showed me to an opening in a chain link fence cut to the exact shape of a human body. The next day on CBS news, the last pictures were of the Iron Curtain on the

Hungarian border being dismantled—a chain link fence cut open to the same shape as in my dream . . . the fence dismantled so that language becomes an opening the body enters freely.

Like this dream of the fence being dismantled, the poems in this book grant us new visions, new stories to carry in the heart. We hope that the poems carry both sorrow and hope to the reader, for they celebrate the worlds found in new countries, new relationships, new landscapes of nature and health.

As we conclude this introduction, we want to thank many people who helped bring this book to life. First, we want to thank Ruth Thorne-Thomsen, the artist whose evocative photograph is on the cover.

Next, we thank five women who worked for Milkweed Editions as volunteers: Loretta Dakin, Deidre Pope, Amy Whitney, and Sheila Gilmartin read hundreds of poems, and spent hours researching this theme in libraries and bookstores. Karen Jersild, our assistant editor, read every poem that arrived and helped with the vision of the book along with the daily paperwork. We thank these women and the staff at Milkweed Editions for believing in the project.

Most of all, we thank the women whose poems are included in this book. We admire their courage, their voices, their drive to create coherence and unity in their lives. Feminism is still the best word to take into account the courage required for a woman to write, to sustain the life of writing as a woman in this culture. We thank the writers for their courage, for doing what Joan Larkin describes in one of her poems:

> I'm climbing this hill,
> I'm picking up
> this pen.

Deborah Keenan
December 1989

Roseann Lloyd
December 1989

——

# Acknowledgements

We thank the following writers and publishers for permission to reprint some of the poems that appear in this anthology.

Teresa Anderson's poem, "Kneading Bread," first appeared in *Sing Heavenly Muse*, Issue 13. Reprinted by permission of the author.

Sophie Cabot Black's poem, "She Drives," first appeared in the Spring 1989 issue of *Field* #40. Reprinted by permission of the author.

Marjorie Agosin's poem, "Disappeared Women I," is from her volume of poetry, *Zones of Pain*, translated by Cola Franzen, published by White Pine Press, 1988. Reprinted by permission of White Pine Press.

Jill Breckenridge's poem, "Bottled," first appeared in *Great River Review*, Volume 6, Number 2, 1985. Reprinted by permission of the author.

Rosario Caicedo's poem, "Nochebuena," originally appeared in *El Taller Literario*, May, 1986. Reprinted by permission of the author.

Kathleen Cain's poem, "The Lesson," was originally published in *Crossing the River*, by The Permanent Press. Reprinted by permission of the author.

Marilyn Chin's poem, "The Administrator," first appeared in *Caliban*, Number 5, ©1988. Reprinted by permission of the author.

Florence Dacey's poem, "Farewell," originally appeared in her volume of poetry *The Necklace*, published by Midwest Villages and Voices Press. Reprinted by permission of the author.

Regina DeCormier-Shekerjian's poem, "The Left Eye of Odin," appeared in *Porch*. "This Spring" is a revised section of "The Instruction of Clotilde," which appeared in *Helicon Nine*. Reprinted by permission of the author.

Diana Der Hovanessian's poem, "Radio Yerevan," was originally published in *How To Choose Your Past*, Ararat Press. Her poems, "Without You I Am" and "At Mt. Auburn Cemetery," are from *About Time*, Ashod Press. Reprinted by permission of the author.

Joan Dobbie's poem, "My First Memory, Switzerland, circa 1947," has appeared in *Poetic Space* and in *Gold Dust*. "Things Grow Up Out Of The Dark" appeared originally in *Pacifica*. Reprinted by permission of the author.

Lorraine Duggin's poem, "For My Mother Who Lives," Section IV, first appeared in *Elkhorn Review*, Fall, 1988. Reprinted by permission of the author.

Rhina Espaillat's poem, "You Call Me By Old Names," first appeared in *Riverside '53*, a collection of poems chosen in competition by W. H. Auden, Marianne Moore, and Karl Shapiro, and published by Haddam House. Reprinted by permission of the author.

Rina Ferrarelli's poem, "Emigrant/Immigrant II," was published originally in *West Branch*, #23. Reprinted by permission of the author.

Brigitte Frase's poem, "Homegoing," originally appeared in *Milkweed Chronicle*, Volume 4, Number 1. Reprinted by permission of the author.

Lucia Cordell Getsi's poem, "Oradour-sur-Glane. Silence.," was originally published in *Prairie Schooner*, Summer, 1989. Reprinted by permission of the author.

Sandra Gilbert's poem, "The Parachutist's Wife," is reprinted from *Blood Pressure* by Sandra M. Gilbert, by permission of W. W. Norton & Company, Inc. Copyright ©1988 by Sandra M. Gilbert.

Carolina Hospital's poem, "The Mother Tongue," first appeared in *The Panhandler*, from the University of West Florida. Reprinted by permission of the author.

Sibyl James' poem, "Shortwave in Shanghai," first appeared in *event*, 1986. Reprinted by permission of the author.

Julia Kasdorf's poem, "Mennonites," first appeared in *West Branch*, #24. "Green Market, New York" first appeared in *The Journal*. Reprinted by permission of the author.

Melanie Kaye/Kantrowitz's poem, "Jerusalem Shadow," was originally published in *The Tribe of Dina: A Jewish Women's Anthology*, Beacon Press (revised and expanded/1989). Reprinted by permission of the author.

Patricia Kirkpatrick's poem, "For A Woman Murdered While Running At Land's End, October 1979," originally appeared in *Learning To Read*, Meadow Press, 1982. Reprinted by permission of the author.

Irena Klepfisz's poem, "Etlekhe verter oyf mame-loshn, A Few words in the mother tongue," appeared in *The Tribe of Dina: A Jewish Women's Anthology*, Beacon Press (revised and expanded/1989). Reprinted by permission of the author.

Jacqueline Lapidus' poem, "Exmatriate," was previously published in *Sinister Wisdom*, and then in her own book *Ultimate Conspiracy*. Reprinted by permission of the author.

---

Meredith Stricker's long poem, "The Lightning Hive," first appeared in *Epoch*, Fall, 1989. We have selected two sections, "bee mother" and "ISLAND" for this anthology. Reprinted by permission of the author.

Stephanie Strickland's poem, "Diringer's *The Alphabet: A Key To The History of Mankind*," first appeared in *Prairie Schooner*, Volume 61, Number 4, Winter, 1987. Reprinted by permission of the author.

Gloria Vando's poem, "Chimayó," first appeared in *Helicon Nine*, Numbers 14/15, 1986. "New York City Mira Mira Blues" appeared in *Stiletto*, Number 1, 1989. Reprinted by permission of the author.

Mitsuye Yamada's poems, "I Learned To Sew," "Obon: Festival of the Dead," and "The Club" are from her book, *Desert Run: Poems and Stories*, Kitchen Table: Women of Color Press, 1988, and are reprinted with permission of the author and publisher. Kitchen Table's address is P.O. Box 908, Latham, New York, 12110.

———

# Looking For Home

## ONE

### *"Voices tie us closer than the printed news..."*

*—Sibyl James, "Short Wave in Shanghai"*

# TWO

## "Say that I am not going back
## I am staying here"

—Mitsuye Yamada, "I Learned To Sew"

## THREE

## "the first words that were mine ..."

—Beverly Acuff Momoi, "Portrait"

# FOUR

## "Not sure of weather or welcome..."

—Marilyn Boe, "Sunday Afternoon at the State Hospital"

# FIVE

## "Then there is earth I say..."

—Christine Dumaine, *"Second Language"*

# SIX

## "On this land, still marked with familiar footprints..."

—Mary Crescenzo Simons, "Return to Mankiller Flats, Oklahoma"

# SEVEN

## "The more a thing is torn, the more places it can connect."

—Meredith Stricker, "ISLAND"

# ONE

"Voices tie us closer
than the printed news..."

—Sibyl James
"Shortwave In Shanghai"

# bee mother

to Èva Ráth Stricker

from a Hungarian dictionary

| | |
|---|---|
| MOTHER | – anya, méh |
| | |
| MÉH | – bee; womb, uterus |
| méhébe fogadni | – to conceive |
| méhallas | – hive, shed |
| méhanya | – uterus |
| méhbaj | – hysteria, fits of the mother |
| méhbefogadás | – conception |
| méhbeli | – uterine |
| méhcsipés | – sting of a bee |
| méhdüh | – uterine fury |
| méhgörcs | – spasms in hysteria |
| méhgörcsös | – hysterical |
| méhgyümölcs | – fruit of the womb |
| méhhas | – bee house, apiary |
| méhhüvely | – vagina |
| méhkirálynö | – queen bee |
| méhkosár | – bee hive |
| méhmagzat | – embryo, fetus |
| méhraj | – swarm of bees |
| méhrajzas | – swarming of bees |
| méhser | – metheglin |
| méhszáj | – mouth of the womb |
| méhnyésztés | – bee farming |
| méhtükör | – speculum |
| méhüszög | – false conception |

Meredith Stricker

in my mother's lost language
it suddenly becomes clear
the hive we are born into
the bee hum
of all languages
we speak or will never hear

.

Meredith Stricker

# The Mother Tongue

A dark cul de sac,
around an island of palms
without exits.
A shadow chases me
and shouts
louder, louder:
"Turncoat, traitor."
I run faster.
It pulls me out of the spiral,
begs me to explain.
I cannot answer.
I have stopped speaking.

Carolina Hospital

# Diringer's The Alphabet:
# A Key to the History Of Mankind

I wanted . . . a guneaform, a woman's form
of writing, and thought perhaps, Cuneiform it, so tactile
the script, the palpable wedges pressed in wet clay;
writing at once, as a fresco is painted—
but in this book, in the pictographs
that underlie Cuneiform, there is only one sign
for woman, pudendum. Slavegirl
and servant, male, also given by genital description.
Man is head, with mouth in it, plus beard.

I thought, apart from the argument made for it here
as sole origin of alphabets, this form
is just one instance. Hieroglyphic determinatives
for man and woman in Egypt look more matched,
both stickfigure-like, kneeling on one foot, one shin.
Except that the woman has longer hair, no arms.
Except there is no difference, for a woman, between
first- and second-person singular. Quietly, here, grammar
instates what marital law and canon teaching on abortion
legislate: I am—not only yours—but you.

Stephanie Strickland

27

I began to wonder whether, somewhere, in the world a different
thinking, different being, existed, and flipping through
the book was struck by Chinese trigrams: elegance,
abstraction. Three lines above each other meant,
the footnote said, sky, and dry, and prime, and creative
grandfather life. Slashed, into six
little lines, the sign meant secondarily
and destruction and foreboding and grandmother and earth.
Later Chinese for a man an upright stroke, hook
projected to the left; for woman a buckling crook, large
bundle at the shoulder; woman next to woman meaning
quarrel—and man next to word meaning true.

I did find, toward the end, one group of people, the Yao
or Miao or Miao-tzu tribe, called
by the Chinese "wild Southern barbarians."
Fifty thousand, in Viet Nam and Laos, before our war.
The Yao had, I found them nowhere else, four
different signs of equal
complication: mother father person heart
—but as I said, wiped out.

Stephanie Strickland

# Etlekhe verter oyf mame-loshn/
# *A few words in the mother tongue*

*lemoshl:*    for example

*di kurve*    the whore
a woman who acknowledges her passions

*di yidene*    the Jewess    the Jewish woman
ignorant    overbearing
let's face it:    every woman is one

*di yente*    the gossip    the busybody
who knows what's what
and is never caught off guard

*di lezbianke*    the one with
a roommate    though we never used
the word

*dos vaybl*    the wife
or the little woman

—

*in der heym*    at home
where she does everything to keep
*yidishkayt*    alive

*yidishkayt*    a way of being
Jewish    always arguable

Irena Klepfisz

in *mark*     where she buys
di *kartofl un khalah*
(yes, potatoes and challah)

di *kartofl*     the physical counter–
part of *yidishkayt*

mit *tsibeles*     with onions
that bring *trern tsu di oygn*
tears to her eyes     when she sees
how little it all is
*veyniker un veyniker*
less and less

di *khalah*     braided
vi *irh hor far der khasene*
like her hair before the wedding
when she was *aza sheyn meydl*
such a pretty girl

di *lange shvartse hor*
the long black hair
di *lange shvartse hor*

———

*a froy kholmt*     a woman
dreams     *ihr ort oyf der velt*
her place in this world
*un zi hot moyre*     and she is afraid
so afraid of the words

Irena Klepfisz

kurve

yidene

yente

lezbianke

vaybl

zi kholmt     she dreams

un zi hot moyre     and she is afraid

ihr ort

di velt

di heym

der mark


a meydl kholmt

a kurve kholmt

a yidene kholmt

a yente kholmt

a lezbianke kholmt


a vaybl kholmt

di kartofl

di khalah


yidishkayt


zi kholmt

di hor

di lange shvartse hor


zi kholmt

zi kholmt

zi kholmt


Irena Klepfisz

# The Space Between

Me fugué del español runaway child.
La mano larga de sus sílabas me envuelve
como chicle de mascar cuyas hebras rosadas
se vuelven a pegar a la suela del zapato.

Lo escojo. Escojo vivir en plena corriente.
Los pies quietos como orejas
vibran con el rozo del agua en el casco de la canoa.
Cada pez, cada rama, cada corcholata
deja su traza de helecho.

The maze of marks that look so foreign
strains my eyes. They are my own "King's English,"
the one I long denied. I speak
their sounds that carry me into the air
and giggle like a drum beat full of bees
or a house of carts children peep round
to look into the mirror
where they set their palms against
those of the mother who turns
into another.

Ana Luisa Ortiz de Montellano

# The Space Between

(translation)

"I'm a runaway child
              left Spanish behind."
The long grasp of its syllables holds me
like chewing gum on a shoe.

I choose Spanish; choose to live in the middle of the stream.
In the middle of the stream my feet like ears
feel the rush of water on the shell.
Each fish, each branch, each bottle cap
leaves a crabbed pattern.

El laberinto de señas tan ajeno
me agota. Es mi propio inglés,
el que tan largo rechacé. Pronuncio
sus sonidos que de plano me desplantan,
me cosquillean como tamborazo rezongando de abejas,
o casa de carretas de donde atisban unos niños,
ven el espejo
en el que ponen las palmas contra las de ella,
la madre que se desmadeja.

Ana Luisa Ortiz de Montellano

33

# Ohio Is the Iroquois Word for Beautiful

*la luna clava en la mar un largo cuerno de luz . . .*
—Federico Garcia Lorca

"The moon is nailed to the 'river'
by a great horn of light. . . ."
eh, Federico?
Great lines live in the mind,
repeat in time, in place,
resonating like radio voices
forever in the vacuum of space.
I looked at my moon nailed
to the Allegheny and thought
of your moon tied to the ocean
on the other side of silence,
our disparate moons nailed into place,
and our identical wishes—
a great cornucopia
flowing into the Ohio.

Helen Ruggieri

# Unspoken World

I sometimes think about
the colder, smaller life
I might have lived

a far latitude
a distant occupation
another language

how I might have stopped
in the middle of a task
forgetting what it was

I had been reaching for
how the eyes of an extinct
animal would shadow me

hungry, amber and full of
more dead worlds than the
plains have grass

and outside that dark
window flightless birds
would mimic languages

I never learned and
mock in plangorous bleats
poems I never wrote

Helen Ruggieri

# Short Wave In Shanghai

I've never felt so knifed loose from the world
as if this country were a world itself
and didn't need the news beyond it. The moon
outside my hotel room seems easier to reach
than anything in English on the short wave.
I turn the small dial slowly
through the bits of voice, half a syllable enough
to know the language isn't mine. Moscow
comes in clear, and the evangelical stations.
Somehow the message is the same.
I search even for the lies of the VOA
with its Yankee Doodle theme.
There are things I learn—
the price of al-u-min-i-um in British tones,
the Armed Forces Network uses only women. One
of these facts is important. But everything
fades in and out, resolves at crucial times
to science fiction sound-effects. Winter mornings
when the sun's not up, there's nothing.
At midnight, sound is clear. The principles
of space and light and voice confuse me.
And the times. The British morning
is my evening. The NASA space ship
bursts now into flames, inside my yesterday.
The distance seems as large as death.

Sibyl James

I've always understood that voices tie us closer
than the printed news. In the dim lights of my room
I wash the dinner dishes at the bath sink,
listening for anything on BBC—the punch
of comedy routines, the price of gold,
the Big Ben chimes. I think it's London
World War II, and the front is somewhere
just past the fading line I hold.

Sibyl James

# Against Simple Reading

to Èva Ráth Stricker


> I have read the lily.
> I cannot read the hare, the chick, the bee.
>
> —H.D.


My mother's hair is a maze I cannot read.
She says maize on the telephone, yellow grain,
like it was in Hungary, not like her hair, dark
and foreign, not the hare she traced on my palm
as a child: merre fut anyulascka:   it ran, it ran
into my hand, it ran into these words, across
eastern borders, across the war, returning words
to fugitive things: vase, lily, shard, innocent
rose, faucet, moonlight on tiles, face.
The ones who can't speak are the safest.
Stairways, horses & plains: anonymous, scattered.
The way television particles detonate the woman,
a woman who is leaning into a place she will forget.
Her image is safe, but lost to her, all particles merged
deeper into the story than its telling, sparing her
and sparing all unvoiced things—their names fled—
against the enemy's decoding, against simple reading.


Meredith Stricker

# You Call Me by Old Names

You call me by old names: how strange
to think of "family" and "blood,"
walking through flakes, up to the knees
in cold and democratic mud.

And suddenly I think of people
dead many centuries ago:
my ancestors, who never knew
the dubious miracle of snow. . . .

Don't say my names, you seem to mock
their charming, foolish, Old World touch—
Call me "immigrant," or Social
Security card such-and-such,
or future citizen, who boasts
two eyes, two ears, a nose, a mouth,
but no names from another life,
a long time back, a long way south.

Rhina Espaillat

# Forked Tongue

for *Lewis Grassic Gibbon, Scottish novelist, 1901–1935*

Celtic tribes speak an anapestic lilt
quite different from Germanic languages—
so the slow strangulation of the Scottish
tongue in the iambic thud taught by the

English schooled masters to the prisoners
of universal education—farm boys and
serving lasses, shopkeeper's children,
learning to speak "correctly" the

proper vowel and consonantal sounds
the conquering rhythm demands.
Thus a tongue becomes divided,
a people broken into two expressions—

one to be thought in, one to be loved,
one for the heart, one for the head.

Helen Ruggieri

# Invisible Boundaries

*While looking at the painting After the Flood by April Gornik.*

*There is nothing one man will not do to another.*
—Carolyn Forché, *The Country Between Us*

*No conozco la palabra* to say I sometimes miss you *en español.*
It is not *malograr* or *fracasar* or *perder.*
I can't find the words in my language or yours.
I keep remembering what Alberto said,
who I am is not affected by this separation
but I get tangled in painful sheets.
*No es dolor, es ensensible!* Nothing is exact.
The suffering is also who I am;
turning stones over and over,
trying to fathom below the surface.
If only we could move freely among molecules—
no separation between stone, water and air.
The invisible boundaries that divide us
also contain the vessels of our children,
even the one we robbed identity and face from.
I struggle with definitions:
go deeper into the idea of word,
primal soup, blue-green algae,
the first "I am" the world uttered.

I've been throwing the *I Ching*, finding beauty
in the physical shape of language and square holes in coins.
It keeps coming up the first hexagram, six unbroken lines.
*Tian.* Origin. Heaven above, heaven below.
Pictures echo the history of words,
the name written in English is a pale shadow.

Maureen Hurley

41

Tian, the ideograph for heaven 天 made from man 人 and
  ⌐ big aspirations.
an, 宀 mountains or a woman 安 with a roof over her head
means all is in order. And the last pictograph,
a double gate 門 made from the sun. 日 Gate of heavenly peace.
Tiananmen. But six dragons are let loose on the world.

So much gets lost in translation—even from English to English.
The distance between ex-lovers, tricked by language
into believing each was something the other was not.
From the Peruvian Andes to the Amazon, the *Apurimac*
is so many syllables falling over stone—
the *apu*, the Inca's holy mountain
and the *rimac*, the singing or talking river,
Unsatisfied with the first metaphor the world made,
we cannot talk to each other.

Someone asks me a question in Russian, I answer in Spanish,
not my native tongue. Language dominance confusion.
When you call, I slip back down the throat of darkness.
Climbing the mountains wasn't enough. When all else failed,
you wanted a madonna/whore to ply you with stinging whips of
    words
but the communion dress in my closet is brittle with age,
the lace and horse's sweat on my thighs is caked with dust.

Maureen Hurley

I learn the Russian word **МИР** is the same for world and peace.
**МОСТ** is a bridge. What happens on the other side of the world
also affects who we are. I am making a bridge of sacred rocks
to the cardinal directions because I was undone by the violence
at Tiananmen Square. I am an artist first; poetry is a translation.
Sometimes, I begin to paint everything red and black
but it tricks me into sky blue and tender lavenders.
People see beauty in my work but I see only death
because I fasten my kimono from right to left
like that of an exquisite corpse.

The birds are trying to move molecules again.
One breaks through the window screen,
the other bounces off glass panes
like bullets ricocheting in Lima, Independence Eve.
I cannot go back to who I was and wait
for the day when it no longer matters.
Long shadows of summer solstice, your name—
one more broken syllable the night whispers.
It's times like this I curse the limitations of gender;
to be nothing more than chattel,
without even a common language between us.
*Respira hondo*, my masseuse advises me,
plying the muscles of the world with sweet oil.
I give back your blue stone heart.
How easily I was replaced by the one
who wears your daughter's face.


*Summer Solstice 1989*


Maureen Hurley

# Freedom

for Belkis Cuza Malé

For 20 years they hid your words
afraid of you,
a young girl from Guantánamo,
the daughter of a cement-factory worker.

They silenced poems of
cinderellas and silver platters,
frightened by your beautiful people
and portraits of sad poets.

Now, far from your island and them;
your poems shout without restrictions.
But the words remain unheard.
"Here, a poem
    doesn't upset anyone."

Carolina Hospital

# About Writing Poetry

Why take time, with so little time left
To thread words into meaning, make wordweavings
When time is running out
When whales are slowly dying
And mushrooms, growing in my beloved mountains
Are full of built-in Caesium-14
When all the pasta primavera, this summer of 1988
At the piazza della signoria
Will be slightly radioactive
When young pregnant women in the old countries
Slide Geiger-counters across their rounded bellies?

Why spend so many precious hours, with so few hours left
Learning the craft of poetry,
Painstakingly, agonizingly slow
Learning to express senses, at a time running insane?

Realists, dealing in hard facts, survivalists
Blast caverns into rock, in sunny California
Stockpile freeze-dried food for fifty years,
Stack rifles with plenty of ammo,
"Dinky Devil" subguns, 32 rounds in two seconds,
Variable perimeter rifles with cyclic rates
Of thirteen thousand rounds per minute.

Should I write poetry, or should I teach a child to pray?
Should I write poetry,
Or should I breed radiation-resistant butterflies
In old shoe-boxes?

Sophie Slingeland

Should I buy the tanned hide of an old elk,
Write one more poem
Write with coal, blackberryjuice and lime
A woman's poem
About the little big things in life
Springleaves, the touch of summerwind, the sound of rushing rivers
The scent of fresh-plowed earth, the color of robins' eggs
And the laughter of a small child's joy?

So, I'll write it on soft leather, shape a vessel of clay
Store it deep down, in a dry cave
Maybe eons later, all long past
A discoverer, looking back centuries
Descending
Will find we once had words.

Sophie Slingeland

# Without You* I Am

| | | |
|---|---|---|
| a lute | without | strings |
| strings | without | knots |
| knots | without | pegs |
| pegs | without | holes |
| holes | without | ground |
| ground | without | seed |
| seed | without | rain |
| rain | without | skies |
| skies | without | wind |
| wind | without | direction |
| direction | without | home |
| home | without | hearth |
| hearth | without | fire |
| fire | without | fuel |
| fuel | without | air |
| air | without | sun |
| sun | without | light |
| light | without | dark |
| dark | without | sound |
| sound | without | melody |
| melody | without | words |
| words | without | heart |
| heart | without | hope |
| hope | without | song |
| song | without | a lute. |

* the Armenian language

Diana Der Hovanessian

# TWO

"Say that I am not going back
I am staying here"

—Mitsuye Yamada
"I Learned To Sew"

# I Learned To Sew

How can I say this?
My child
My life is nothing
There is nothing to tell

My family in Japan was too poor
to send me to school
I learned to sew
always I worked to help my family
when I was seventeen years old
and no one made marriage offer
a friend in our village who was going
to Hawaii a picture bride
said to me
Come with me.

I did not want to
my parents did not want me to
my picture was sent to a stranger anyway
a young man's photograph and letter came
I was already seventeen years old
I went to the island of Hawaii to marry
this photograph.

This man came to the boat
he was too shy to talk to me
the Immigration man said to him
Here
sign here for her
He walked away
The Immigration man came to me
Don't you have relatives in Hawaii?

Mitsuye Yamada

I said
Yes I have that man who will marry me
He said
Go back to Japan on the next boat
I said
I will wait here for my man
The Immigration man said
No
your man is not coming back
he told me he does not want you
he said you are too ugly for him
why don't you go back to Japan
on the next boat?
I said
No
I am not going back
I am staying here

    Just
    A minute
    My child
    Put that pen down
    Do not write this
    I never told this to anybody
    Not even to my oldest son, your father
    I now tell this story
    To you first time in sixty years

Mitsuye Yamada

I sat at Immigration for a long time
people came and people went
I stayed
I could not see the sky
I could not see the sun
outside the window
I saw a seaweed forest
the crickets made scraping sounds
the geckos went tuk tuk tuk
sometimes a gecko would come into my room
but I was not afraid to talk to it
it came and it went as it pleased.

I was thinking about Urashima Taro
you know the story?
Urashima disappeared into the sea
lived in the undersea world
married a beautiful princess
returned to his village
a very old man
I was thinking
I will leave this place
only when I am an old lady.

Pretty soon the Immigration man came to me
We found your cousin
In two weeks a cousin I met once
in Japan came for me
I stayed with him and his wife until
my cousin found a job for me
I worked doing housework
I did this for one year.

Mitsuye Yamada

My cousin found a husband for me
he was a merchant
we had a small store
and sold dry goods
my husband died after three sons
your father, my oldest son, was six years old
I could not keep the store
I could not read
I could not write
the only thing I knew how to do was sew.

I took the cloth from our store
sewed pants and undergarments
put the garments on a wooden cart
*ombu* the baby on my back
we went from plantation to plantation
sold my garments to the workers
I was their only store
sewed more garments at night
I did this for five years.

Your father grew up to love study and books
my friends called him the professor
he was then eleven years old
I said to him you need a father
He said I want to go to college
I said to him I will marry any man you say
I will marry any man
who will send you to college.

Mitsuye Yamada

One day he came home and said
I went to a matchmaker and
found a husband for you
he will marry a widow with three sons
will send them to college
he is a plantation foreman.

I married this man.

By and by my oldest son went away
to college in Honolulu
but my husband's boss told him
I need workers
your three sons must work
on my plantation like the others.
My husband said
No
He kept his word to my oldest son
and lost his job.

After that we had many hard times
I am nothing
know nothing
I only know how to sew
I now sew for my children and grandchildren
I turn to the sun every day of my life
pray to Amaterasu Omikami
for the health and
education of my children
for me that is enough

Mitsuye Yamada

My child
Write this
There      take your pen
There      write it
Say that I am not going back
I am staying here

Mitsuye Yamada

# Learning My Father's Language

*The accent is always on the first syllable:*
*in the word of more than three syllables,*
*there is a secondary accent on the third syllable.*

*——Instructional Manual In Czech*

He tells me about the time
his schoolmates laugh so hard,
laugh him under the desk, red-faced,
out of the room, embarrassed, down
the halls, humiliated,
of Jungmann School.

First generation American son
of Bohemian immigrants,
how was he to know

this language of different rules,
this country which found
humor in foreignness,
this vocabulary ludicrous

when accent falls upon
*em*, as in "emigré," which
his parents are, or "eminent,"
which they aren't,

accent falling again on *gen*
as in "gentle" or "gentlemen,"
neither of which howling
classmates pretend to be

Lorraine Duggin

when the boy who becomes my father
sounds out, broken, aloud,
pronouncing from his first year
reader a word he sees on the page:

em′-er-gen′-cy.

Lorraine Duggin

# Poem for My Grandmother's Grandmother

I

Minukha, Minukha, here comes your Faigl's Rukhl
running across the bridge from Russia
to Poland into your open arms.
*Bubbe, ikh vil a fingerl, a shayn fingerl*
your Faigl's Rukhl would say, as she squirmed
in your lap reaching for the rings
the pretty rings you sold in the marketplace
gold-filled rings set with bits of colored glass.
*Nayn Mamela du kenst nit hobn a fingerl*
you would say, for those rings became eggs and cheese
milk and *challah*, a woolen blanket for your lap
a roof over your shaved and *sheytled* head.
But one day Minukha, when your Rukhl
your Faigl's Rukhele came flying
over the bridge on her fat little legs
you held her tightly on your lap and you said
*Nem Mamela nem a fingerl nem a shayn fingerl*
*nem dos shaynste fingerl in der gantser velt.*
Rukhl clapped her hands and picked out a ring
a pretty ring a gold-filled ring set with bits of red glass
red glass that shone in the sun
like the flames of Faigl's candles
on her beloved *Shabbos*
red glass that shone
like the flames that were to burn up the bridge
to your little Polish town
red glass that shone
like the flames that were to burn up
your beloved *shvester* Chaya and your beloved *shvester* Golda
under the Nazis hands in the years to come

Lesléa Newman

58

Oy Minukha how the tears fell from your eyes that day
as though you knew what was to be
when you placed the ring   the pretty ring
the gold-filled ring set with bits of colored glass
into Rukhl's tiny hand before you sent her back
over the bridge from Poland to Russia
to America, standing on a big ship
with one *klayn henteleh* holding tight to her *Mame*
her other hand holding the ring
the pretty ring   the ring from her *Bubbe*
the gold-filled ring set with bits of red glass
*dos fingerl   dos shayn fingerl*
*dos shaynste fingerl in der gantser velt.*

       II

Minukha, Minukha, I never knew your name
until yesterday   yesterday when I sat with your Rukhl
your Faigl's Rukhl   and I said to her
*Bubbe, kh vil a meiseh   ikh vil a Bubbe Meiseh*
*Bubbe, du gedenkst deyn Bubbe?*
And my grandma Ruthie, your granddaughter Rukhl
shut her eyes as her mind flew across the bridge
from Brooklyn to Russia to Poland
to visit a little town that no longer exists.
*Meyn bubbe, ikh gedenk nit meyn bubbe,* she said,
no, *Mamela,* my grandmother I don't remember.
She opened her eyes to see my eyes,
dark brown like her own, filling with tears.
Then she took my hand Minukha
and she said wait, wait a minute
rings, rings she sold in the marketplace

Lesléa Newman

gold-filled rings set with bits of colored glass.
My *shvester* Tzivia named her oldest for my *bubbe*,
Minnie, Minnie her name was.
Say it in Jewish, Grandma.
In Jewish? In Jewish it would be Minukha
now you know your great-great grandmother's name,
alright already enough with the crying
*oy Mamela*, such a *shayna maideleh* you are
but always the tears are falling from your eyes.
Come, we'll go down for supper.
And so Minukha, down to eat we went
and then I kissed my grandma Ruthie
your granddaughter Rukhl
and left her nursing home with a gift
a gift more precious than a ring
even a gold-filled ring set with bits of red glass
lost long ago
a gift of a name no longer forgotten
a name to whisper into the darkness
when I am alone and afraid
a name to chant on the *Shabbos*
or sing aloud on the Holy days
a name to turn to in times of trouble
Oy Minukha, what would you have done?
a name to wrap around my heart
like a string around my finger
or a ring or a *fingerl* so I shouldn't forget
a name to shout to the world
a name to sing like a lullaby
a name that means to rest
Minukha      Minukha      Minukha

Leslèa Newman

# Emigrant/Immigrant I

From the people
beyond reckoning of generations
a town whose customs and tongue
defined you as much as your name
your occupation.

But you're adaptable.
You stand alone in your new country
your new town, the old one
an obscure allusion
with a newly-minted
easier-to-pronounce name,
given or chosen,
new clothes
and the latest American haircut.

Neither color, nor shape or size,
nor the face you were born with
can you take for granted anymore.
People talk around you
point things out
syl-lab-i-cate slowly
or raise their voices
but you smile, grateful,
eager to please.
You're learning to read lips
they're helping you cross the street.
YOU, who are you?
They don't know, do you?

Rina Ferrarelli

# Emigrant/Immigrant II

A slight accent.
      Forming
each phrase before
delivery
and never a slur.

Checking
      every move,
prepared
for all contingencies.
      Close,
yet not quite.

      Insisting
on a knife and fork
when your fingers
would do as well.

Almost there.
The place sighted,
but out of reach.
Destined never to cross

into the interior.
A bridge, a border town.

Rina Ferrarelli

# Babouchka

Now, does she still want to live?
Her voice had drifted, travelled up into space
Beamed through satellite dishes
Across the mountains
Across the oceans
Through the plains and rivers,
Turning more brittle with each mile.

I am sipping black TCHAI with sugar,
It is four in the morning.
My cold fingers wrap around the cup,
Thick colorful terracotta,
Made by hands in Italy.
Italy
Springbreak, Lake Como, Palmtrees
Camellias blooming in old gardens
Statues of mournful stone maidens, holding urns
Mimosatrees, fragrant puffy little yellow flowers
Dusted with melancholic ancient fragrance
Leaves that fold
Like praying hands
At the slightest touch
Italy—
Under a striped umbrella
Lovely silk blouses
Embroidered by women in Sicily
Who hunched under twisted figtrees
Hard, calloused hands
Gently stitching, with the sweet smell of rotting fruit.

Sophie Slingeland

Un *Gelato, Gelati, Gelatini*
Gelati dripping into my pink summerdress.
*Villa Carlotta, Tremezzo, Va bene*
*Bon giorno, Bellissima, Ciao*
*La vita*
Grandmother wears laceknit gloves and a white hat.
Palmtrees rustling. We both love Italy, *Gelati* and *Panettone*,
The sound of bells drifting down from the nearest *campanile*.

I am tired of living she said
Tired of walking
Tired of reading
Tired of waiting. All my friends have died. I am eighty-eight.

I want to sound cheerful, talk of daffodils
About to bloom in my garden.
It is still snowing, I say.
Just like in Russia, she whispers—
No mountains here. The lakes are thawing. My lilacs have buds.
A deer has nibbled bark of the birchtree.
The winters are long here . . .
Just like in Russia.

Sophie Slingeland

I am tired of living she says, with the voice of a little girl.
Yesterday she fell, lay there waiting,
A bird with a broken wing.
So here I am. Listening to time.
Is it her time? Or will they save her?
Again?
So she can be
Our memories, our scrapbook of the past
Softened by a thousand hours.
Less harsh
More beautiful
Or
Can we let her go,
Let her go with her dreams yet unlived?

Sophie Slingeland

# Mennonites

We keep our quilts in closets and do not dance.
We hoe thistles along fence rows for fear
we may not be perfect as our Heavenly Father.
We clean up his disasters. No one has to
call; we just show up in the wake of tornadoes
with hammers, after floods with buckets.
Like Jesus, the servant, we wash each other's feet
twice a year and eat the Lord's Supper,
afraid of sins hidden so deep in our organs
they could damn us unawares,
swallowing this bread, his body, this juice.
Growing up, we love the engravings in Martyr's Mirror:
men drowned like cats in burlap sacks,
the Catholic inquisitors,
the woman who handed a pear to her son,
her tongue screwed to the roof of her mouth
to keep her from singing hymns while she burned.
We love Catherine the Great and the rich tracts
she gave us in the Ukraine, bright green winter wheat,
the Cossacks who torched it, and Stalin
who starved our cousins while wheat rotted
in granaries. We must love our enemies.
We must forgive as our sins are forgiven,
our great uncle tells us, showing the chain
and ball in a cage whittled from one block of wood
while he was in prison for refusing to shoulder
a gun. He shows the clipping from 1916:
"Mennonites are German milksops, too yellow to fight."

Julia Kasdorf

We love those Nazi soldiers, who, like Moses,
led the last cattle cars rocking out of the Ukraine,
crammed with parents—children then—

learning the names of Kansas, Saskatchewan, Paraguay.
This is why we cannot leave the beliefs
or what else would we be? Why we eat
til we're drunk on shoo-fly and moon pies and borscht.
We do not drink; we sing. Unaccompanied on Sundays,
those hymns in four parts, our voices lift with such force
that we lift, as chaff lifts, toward God.

Julia Kasdorf

# Raid on a Cheyenne Village

Death was lovely.
The tipis burning.
The screams of women like wild birds.
The flare of tipi linings
painted with geometric power signs.
I still can see the orange blaze
of long-tailed warbonnets—
the flames of feathers in flight.
Ghost shirts melting into the unseen world.
Beaded cradleboards,
hair-pipe breastplates,
otter skin shawls.
Then I felt the prick of beading needles.
I howled like a wolf
as the flames touched my legs.
The dead leaves crackled
like fire in the sap of lodge-poles
when I ran into the woods.
All was lost
after the raid of Genèral Mackinzie
in the Freezing Moon.
What I remember
was the smell of burning hair
and the open door of the sky—
the first step I took into the clouds.
What could be lovelier than the fire—
oak yellow, orange
red as life?

Diane Glancy

# Radio Yerevan

Since 1915
the walled monastery
in Jerusalem's Old City
(Vank of the Armenian Church)
has been peopled by
families, exiled by Turks,
each in a room, but now
comfortably.
In a cell warmed with
books and rugs
you will eat cheese,
drink tea and discuss Keats
and Kierkegaard
with a hospitable priest.
Then at ten, someone will tune
the radio to a band marked in green,
for folk songs from the Caucasus.
Stone walls and books
fade to wind and
your father's voice will
cross the years
of your American childhood.
And suddenly
so far from home
his happy child
will inherit all his tears.

Diana Der Hovanessian

# The Lesson

*for my great uncle John Crawford, still in exile from Ballylanders*


Pride got passed at the breakfast table
along with the toast and the eggs.
It was served up cold.
It rolled in on high waves.
It got caught in the undertow of the brogue.

I thought we were in for an early story.
When I hammered at my hard-boiled egg
he said

> that's good, that's good—
> eat it all, eat it all.

1916. Something called a Rising.
I slid the egg out of its shell,
held the toast suspended.
I was only eleven. Just getting breasts.
I couldn't, even with my eyes closed,
imagine 1916. By the time I opened
them, I knew he was talking about war.
All the men in our family
have been in a war at some time or another.
Now it was exile. No going back.

> exile is just too much talk that raises visions
> anyway

he said


Kathleen Cain

I can remember my mother
and the yellow corn meal
that came to Ireland
all the way from Minnesota . . .

I finished my toast
while he talked about the Black and Tans.
They sounded like the Nazis to me.

No. He said. Worse.
Worse.

Kathleen Cain

# Plantings

Everywhere
they go
they plant

their garden
of
bitter melon

odd
shaped
eggplant

red
fat
tomato

ginger
and
white onion

all around
bordering the edges
of their yard

delicacies
of
greentops

banana stalk
leaves'
spread fans—

*Catalina Cariaga*

plantings of no purpose
but to sway
tall and wild

with
bamboo
in the night air

reminding them
of the islands—
behind our home

food first,
and then, symbols
of prosperities

gardenias
and birds
of paradise.

*Catalina Cariaga*

# Elinor Frost's Marble-topped Kneading Table

Imagine that motion, the turning and pressing,
the constant folding and overlapping, the dough
swallowing and swallowing and swallowing itself
again, just as the sea, bellying up the hard shore,
draws back under its own next forward-moving
roll, slides out from under itself
along the beach and back again; that first
motion, I mean, like the initial act
of any ovum (falcon, leopard, crab) turning
into itself, taking all of its outside surfaces
inward; the same circular mixing and churning
and straightening out again seen at the core
of thunderheads born above deserts; that involution
ritualized inside amaryllis bulbs
and castor beans in May.

Regard those hands now, if you never
noticed before, flour-caked fists and palms knuckling
the lump, gathering, dividing, tucking
and rolling, smoothing, reversing. I know,
from the stirring and sinking habits
of your own passions, that you recognize
this motion.

Pattiann Rogers

And far in the distance (you may even
have guessed), far past Orion and Magellan's vapors,
past the dark nebulae and the sifted rings
of interstellar dust, way beyond mass and propulsion,
before the first wheels and orbits of sleep
and awareness, there, inside that moment
which comes to be, when we remember,
at the only center where it has always been,
an aproned figure stands kneading, ripe
with yeast, her children at her skirts.
Now and then she pauses, bends quickly,
clangs open the door, tosses another stick
on the fire.

The Frost Place
Summer, 1987

Pattiann Rogers

# The Silos

All week she watched
the silo grow from concrete staves.
He had to have it,
this seventh silo—
(each one larger than the last).
And now they line one side of the drive,
half-circling the old house
with a great question
she dares not ask.

That house
with its drafty kitchen and slant floors—
nothing but a shelter for the night
when no work can be done.
(Real time spent with machines.)
He said, when they were married,
eighteen years ago this spring,
he'd tear its boards to shedwood and kindling,
build her a real home
on the wooded knoll.

But now that hill is planted
straight in corn
rows up one side and down
and as the sky fades,
fragile as a broken
robin's egg,
silos loom around her
like black corridors
a woman could get lost in.

Nancy Paddock

# The Left Eye of Odin

*for my mother*


She knows them all. Urchins. Beggars
on crutches trundling downhill.
Fools peddling dreams.
The dogfaced baboons of fear. Treasonous
raconteurs—mummers, all of them.
This morning, the sun waits, tangled
like a goat, or a virgin, in the thicket.

—

The braided loaves of bread keep warm
on the table, shrouded in white linen.
She walks away from the table
and stands at the window facing
the garden, which is, she thinks, where
she always stands. There is a sound
of clocks, something else
coming up through the floorboards. Perhaps
it is her father singing the smörgåsbord
menu to the dead. She stuffs her ears

Regina deCormier-Shekerjian

with runes she hauled from the stone
mouths of Sweden, hauled all the way
over the bristling Atlantic
and over the Berkshires to the shores
of the Hudson. The wrong words were
stuck in her mouth, bits of salt
herring and schnapps in her father's mustache
which hung, twitching, over his unruly
mouth. Remember, he said, the sun
is the left eye of Odin and the hands of Odin
know the green limbs of Yggdrasil.

She hides her hand, the one with the twisted
finger, in the pocket of the apron.
The piano has needed tuning for seven years.
Ten years. She does not know
how to survive this day. Her hand gropes
in the empty pocket. She tears the sun
from its nail in the sky, and moves away
from the window.
And watches them come.

—

Regina deCormier-Shekerjian

In twos and threes, the mummers come.
Their shoes on fire, mouse-bitten masks, tin
trumpets and drums. Bells of antimony
ring their legs, their velvet arms
coaxing bears. The bears perform, dragging
their heavy shadows around the circle.
Ropes, red ropes of spittle embroider
the circle. Their eyes go small. Their eyes
measure the circle. The mummers

—

dance. She tips her hat and their randy tongues
go slack with joy. The Fool, a purple
tulip in his mouth, waves his stick, shakes
his bag behind their backs. They are stealing
the maps. And the horses, all the runic knots
hidden in the drawers above the bed.
Their gloved hands are swift, and unerring; one
gold tooth each hangs out to shine.
"Tell the truth, and run," they say. And
wave. And smile their gold. She turns

Regina deCormier-Shekerjian

away. The bears stand, tailless; their circle
a dark forest. There is a moon, a crescent moon
engraved in the middle of the forehead
of the tallest. He turns, they turn, taking
the circle, their ropes of red. They walk upright, up
over the humpback bridge of the sky, their fur
thick with light, their feet soft
unmistakable goodbyes.

—

The earth pivots on its axis, leans
toward the sun. The sun
sighs, spinning and dancing
to the applause of planets, the shifting
impulses. Insequential desires knot
her hands. She rubs her hands. She mutters
a Swedish word, and pulls the shrouds
from the risen bread. Outside,
in the garden, a bird rings the bell
of sky.

Regina deCormier-Shekerjian

# At Mt. Auburn Cemetery

*Defense Secretary Weinberger fears acknowledging
genocide by Turks will offend them.*


My father is lying in a green
field, green, green under a sun
so hot the yellow wheat and pale
straw have turned green in his eyes.
He closes them. He is fifteen.
The green field is in Armenia.
The sun is the Armenian sun
of 1915. He closes his eyes
and seventy years have passed.
I am lying in a green field
in Massachusetts under a sun
so hot it has turned the yellow
weeds green inside my eyes.
I close them tighter and the entire
field turns red. I touch it
with blind fingers. It is not wet
with either blood or tears
like his fields. "Hairig,"
I say, "I am so sorry.
What can I do? How can I talk to you
when this soil that gave you haven
and home with its government
says you never existed.
What can I say, I who therefore
cannot be here to say it?"


Diana Der Hovanessian

# Racial Memories

Dinah Shore sings of America
and Chevrolets
and my mother, whose hands
are beautiful, sits next to me sewing.

I am very young
and even without knowing the word Semite
know that Mama is unfashionable.

My mother sings—better than Dinah Shore,
better than Grama who regrets this daughter's
wooly hair and shadowy moustache; she cannot
walk across the room without her glasses
though she sews a fine hand.

My father only sings when he is drunk on Schubert.
My father is blonde and pale-eyed. His shoulders are broad,
his cranium packed near to bursting: he and I believe
we are German.

Mama agrees with this, except when she and I are alone
we talk of gypsy wagons and Mediterranean heat,
the peppery speech of a land of slivovitz and goulash.
She wears red and grows very dark in the sun. I peel

from my nose down, in dry pink shreds
and in a while *kann Deutsch sprechen.*
It is this and not a Chevrolet convertible that separates me
from my mother as her hands grow crepey. I become my father's

Elizabeth Mische John

child, and never think to ask, *bist du mude? Hast du Schaden?*
When all the boys I dance with are thin, dark-eyed, she is stung
by my rejection of everything she knows to be true: the beautiful
are blonde.

Elizabeth Mische John

# The Grand Tradition of Western Culture

*. . . the Jewess has a well-defined function in even the most serious novels.
Frequently violated or beaten, she sometimes succeeds in escaping dishonor
by means of death, but this is a form of justice; and those who keep their virtue
are docile servants or humiliated women in love with indifferent Christians
who marry Aryan women.*

—Sartre, *Anti-Semite and Jew*


My girlhood was surrounded by flickering screens,
by rows and rows of books
about adored blonde Gentile girls and evil dark girls.
The hero always dumps the dark girl for the blonde.
I was a little dark Jewish ghost
no one would ever fall in love with,
I was killed off a hundred times in massacres.
A ghost hovering in the aisles of movies and libraries.

In the *Jazz Singer*, that great movie hit,
I saw the Jewish boy paint himself with blackface,
sing black folks' songs to white folks,
become rich and famous enough to marry a blonde Gentile girl,
generations of movie moguls became rich enough from these
    movies
to marry blonde Gentile girls.

Julia Stein

These movies follow the Grand Tradition of Western Culture,
—Jewish girls are only good for
rape, massacre, abandonment, humiliation—
a hallowed European tradition culminating in the Feldwhoren,
Fieldwhores for the Nazis,
some beautiful Jewish girls were not immediately gassed,
instead set aside for forced prostitution,
many killed themselves rather than endure it.

Their ghosts haunt
the Grand Tradition of Western Culture,
whenever the movies are played, the books are read
their ghosts from the death camps
will be in the aisles and rooms screaming.

Julia Stein

# The Alphabet by the Pool on a Sunday Afternoon

My mother crawled with the rest,
caught her first breath
out of a dark hole.
Gothic Krakow silent, familiar,
broken into pieces without sense, form.
The "l" in Polish, a sound of pain,
an alphabet in letters
before she put meaning to the first word.

She rose as gulls rise
above public dumps.
Bit by scavenged bit
she built a nest, suburban Connecticut
where the ground
holds swimming pools as mirrors.
The peony is opulent
and ready to explode
its countless red tongues
across these watered lawns.
Gypsy moths embalm the sycamores.
The sound of their eating
is like rain
that never hits the earth.
The sun is a hot breath
relinquishing all thought
to a jet stream engraving "Dutra's Market"
in a large arc of sky.

Lusia Slomkowska

When she moves
it's in her own damped motion,
her footsteps disappearing,
the grid of her body
imprinted on the chaise lounge,
the gas grill branding splits of meat,
smoke rising
through the singed lace of leaves.

Nothing is contained here,
not like history:
the painted egg it handed her
to be locked in the china closet,
away from a handled present,
the clumsy future.
The flowers, the figures
are coddled in crystal
and dust covers the holes
where someone once, very carefully,
put their lips to a straw
and blew the insides out.

Lusia Slomkowska

# The Women I Knew

i

At thirteen I was reading *Oedipus Rex*
and watching Let's Make A Deal.

It was late summer . . .
humid afternoons
frantic
flies in honey
wings
drowning in amber. I

did not do the things
a girl should do.

When jagged pins hooked two hollow eyes
I looked above the page to catch

three women dressed as blue
berries cry and cling to Monty as if
he were a god, and they
his poor disciples who
had just discovered eternal
secrets hidden behind
door #2.

Outside my window I heard
the snap of double-dutch
jump—a city game

Lois Roma-Deeley

the black girls played.
Many times I tried
to duck into the swaying whips
which arched high and pure
above my head like some revolving
door to heaven, my feet
much too white,
too confused,
could not count the beats.

As ropes coiled my ankles,
one hopeless tangle,
the black girls sighed and I

knew enough
to leave.

ii

Coming to a new country
Arriving as a new century
weaned itself from the dead,
my grandmother, just
thirteen, makes her maiden
voyage. She leans on the sleek
oak handrail
of an old ocean steamer
heading for the harbor, sees
fireworks soften the sky and land
near her feet—bursting open
as a flower of light

Lois Roma-Deeley

momentary and alone.
*This honors me,*
she thinks but later
coming ashore, she is told
just the Fourth of July.

She grew old
in my mother's house
and did not smile much,
but made it her daily occupation
to guard the streets with her eyes.

On Saturdays she asks for help
in washing. Though she tries
to hide, I see
the scooped out place
where her breasts had been
and how the muscle twists
clear near the bone.
She does not speak
except to command.

Next I fix her hair,
under the thinning gray
a thick scar careens down
her skull, where
her father cracked
her head
wide open
with the tip
of his silver cane.

Lois Roma-Deeley

He was from the old school
and believed a woman
was hardly good
for nothing.

She deceived him:

At night she takes her knitting
and says she is visiting a friend;

goes instead to school

to read
and write

The new way. The American Way.

But he follows her, beats her

and for more than seventy years

she keeps her silence.

iii

World War II explodes and four women change
their names.
        Maria becomes Mae.
        Concetta is pretty
                Kitty
        Frances wants Fay
        Giuseppina takes

Lois Roma-Deeley

whatever she likes. Sometimes
she is Joan
blood polish and netted hose
two snakes crawl up her back. Black sequin mouths
say: You are rich, from Scarsdale, and
very shrewd.

Then her mood prefers
*Louise*
in a Japanese garden, lilting over
snapdragons,
stem and stamen:
One kiss
and she's gone
becomes Dawn for

ever inside without doors
without tears, at odd
angles to the floor, she

falls over and over
again and again
slipping through cracks
into a new world
which needs no name, only

rough landmarks
to star the way

back.

Lois Roma-Deeley

# Heirloom

My great-grandmother's native
American eyes stare back
At me from a tintype,
She kneels in her garden,
"The most dedicated Christian
I ever knew," my grandfather said
Of her, this ancestor who left
The reservation, her people to marry
The circuit rider, how often did she
Sit in a pew among white people
With that same careful lack
Of a smile, a woman
Who even at eighty had
To keep her long hair tightly
Bound among flowers, I remember
Once I walked with a boy
Through sunset down a Swiss Alp
We had climbed.
We ate wild berries.
They stained our mouths and
What did the woman who
Now stares back at her
Great-granddaughter feel as
She walked, dark hair swaying
To meet the preacher,
How many children, how many
Stony-eyed silences from the congregation
Before her face closed down.

Cinda Thompson

And this woman too
Become the best
Wife, Christian mother
Her son would ever wish
To know. . .

Cinda Thompson

# Burial

I

They have fenced in the dirt road
that once led to Wards Chapel
A.M.E. church,
and cows graze
among the stones that
mark my family's graves.
The massive oak is gone
from out the churchyard,
but the giant space is left
unfilled;
despite the two-lane blacktop
that slides across
the old, unalterable
roots.


II

Today I bring my own child here;
to this place where my father's
grandmother rests undisturbed
beneath the Georgia sun,
above her the neatstepping hooves
of cattle.
Here the graves soon grow back into the land.
Have been known to sink. To drop open without
warning. To cover themselves with wild ivy,
blackberries. Bittersweet and sage.

*Alice Walker*

No one knows why. No one asks.
When Burning Off Day comes, as it does
some years,
the graves are haphazardly cleared and snakes
hacked to death and burned sizzling
in the brush . . .The odor of smoke, oak
leaves, honeysuckle.
Forgetful of geographic resolutions as birds,
the farflung young fly South to bury
the old dead.


III

The old women move quietly up
and touch Sis Rachel's face.
"Tell Jesus I'm coming," they say.
"Tell Him I ain't goin' to be
long."

My grandfather turns his creaking head
away from the lavender box.
He does not cry. But looks afraid.
For years he called her "Woman";
shortened over the decades to
"Oman."
On the cut stone for "Oman's" grave
he did not notice
they had misspelled her name.
(The stone reads *Racher Walker*—not "Rachel"—
*Loving Wife, Devoted Mother.*)

*Alice Walker*

IV

As a young woman, who had known her? Tripping
eagerly, "loving wife," to my grandfather's
bed. Not pretty, but serviceable. A hard
worker, with rough, moist hands. Her own two
babies dead before she came.
*Came to seven children.*
*To aprons and sweat.*
*Came to quiltmaking.*
*Came to canning and vegetable gardens*
*big as fields.*
*Came to fields to plow.*
*Cotton to chop.*
*Potatoes to dig.*
*Came to multiple measles, chickenpox,*
*and croup.*
*Came to water from springs.*
*Came to leaning houses one story high.*
*Came to rivalries. Saturday night battles.*
*Came to straightened hair, Noxzema, and*
*feet washing at the Hardshell Baptist church.*
*Came to zinnias around the woodpile.*
*Came to grandchildren not of her blood*
*whom she taught to dip snuff without*
*sneezing.*

*Alice Walker*

———

Came to death blank, forgetful of it all.

When he called her "Oman" she no longer
listened. Or heard, or knew, or felt.


V

It is not until I see my first-grade teacher
review her body that I cry.
Not for the dead, but for the gray in my
first-grade teacher's hair. For memories
of before I was born, when teacher and
grandmother loved each other; and later
above the ducks made of soap and the orange-
legged chicks Miss Reynolds drew over
my own small hand
on paper with wide blue lines.


VI

Not for the dead, but for memories. None of
them sad. But seen from the angle of her
death.


———
*Alice Walker*

# THREE

"the first words that were mine . . ."

—Beverly Acuff Momoi
"Portrait"

# Exile

The train started to take off
my father's waving hand
stuck in the air—
we run to the window to see
the last scenery of the land
I was born
the last look of the loved ones. . .
It was a crowded train
emotionally unstable people
quizzed together
group of people who had to cut off
what's mean life to them
who had to go away to the unknown—
the air was heavy    children's cry    body smell
they was talking on a high exciting voices
some of us just sat and looked in the dark.
We started to eat the chicken my mother made
it was hard to swallow I had butterfly in my
stomach—
We found a flowery napkin had the smell of
home. . .
My little son's trustful look hanged on me
his warm hand hold mine.
Two people started to argue one of them stated
that a millionaire uncle waiting for him in America
the other one doubt it a lot
they almost hit each other. A little old woman
stop them: "Let him talk about the rich uncle
doesn't cost any money"

Marta Fenyves

It became silence. Some of us fall a sleep some are
just stared each other
the faster and faster running train's rhythm repeated
what—will—tomorrow—bring—

                    what—will—tomorrow—
                    bring—

Marta Fenyves

# Disappeared Woman I

translated by Cola Franzen

I am the disappeared woman,
in a country grown dark,
silenced by the
wrathful cubbyholes
of those with no memory.
You still don't see me?
You still don't hear me
in those peregrinations
through the dense smoke
of terror?
Look at me,
nights, days, soundless tomorrows
sing me
so that no one may
threaten me
call me
to give me back
name,
sounds,
a covering of skin
by naming me.

Don't conspire with
oblivion,
tear down the silence.
I want to be
the appeared woman
from among the labyrinths
come back, return
name myself.
Call my name.

Marjorie Agosin

# A New Refugee

stands
outside my door this morning.
He is an exterminator,
wanting to work.
He is from Havana,
(our province),
with no regrets about having left.

I've seen him
selling limes and newspapers,
I've seen him pushing carts
with snowcones,
I have seen his bent shoulders,
him eating beneath a tree
with a hunger that is not
from here.

Countryman. Stranger.
You are my father twenty years ago.
Come in. Have lunch. In this house
we are not without a gun.

*Marisella Veiga*

# Green Market, New York

The first day of false spring, I hit the street
buoyant, my coat open. I could keep walking
and leave that job without cleaning my desk.
At Union Square the country people slouch
by crates of last fall's potatoes.
An Amish lady tends her table of pies.
I ask where her farm is. Upstate, she says,
but we moved from P.A. where the land is better,
and the growing season's longer by a month.
I ask where in P.A.   A town you wouldn't know,
around Mifflinburg, around Belleville.
And I tell her I was born there.
Now who would your grandparents be?
Thomas and Vesta Peachey.
Well, I was a Peachey, she says
and she grins like she sees the whole farm
on my face. What a place your folks had,
down Locust Grove. Do you know my father,
the harness shop on the Front Mountain Road?
I do. And then we can't think what to say
that Valley so far from the traffic on Broadway.
I choose a pie while she eyes my short hair
then looks square on my face. She knows
I know better than to pay six dollars for this.
Do you live in the city? she asks, do you like it?

Julia Kasdorf

I say no. And that was no lie, Emma Peachey.
I don't like New York, but sometimes these streets
hold me as hard as we're held by rich earth.
I have not forgotten that Bible verse:
Whoever puts his hand to the plow and looks back
is not fit for the kingdom of God.

Julia Kasdorf

# Homegoing

*In the longing that starts one on the path is a kind of*
*homesickness, and some way, on this journey, I have started home.*
*Homegoing is the purpose of my practice.*
  —Peter Matthiessen, *The Snow Leopard*


Hoboken was the first stop
after we stared, fulfilling the duty
of immigrants,
at the six a.m. smudge of Manhattan.
Home, my father said finally,
a year or two later.
We still clung to the eastern shore.
When I walked on the beach
or in the fenced back yard
among the rented forsythia,
staring at anthills in sidewalk cracks
or at invisible Europe on the horizon,
I didn't know—were they part of it?
Home. The sound went by too fast,
an express train with no local stops,
unlike *Heimat*, with rolling diphthongs.
Onset, pause, continuation
with time to climb in and be rocked in its motion.

Brigitte Frase

As a child, exploring
a river bank, I turned a grass blade
over and over, discovering
how attention will coax out
the strangeness lurking in all things.
I waited for something enormous to happen,
sure that the world meant
to confide itself in me.
A deep, rich word, my secret name,
was unbearably close and seemed to be murmuring.
Now, I thought, it will break over me.
"God," I said aloud, interrupting the gathering,
and a door and a world slammed.
I heard only my own voice lost
in natural sounds.
I was alone in a field by a river.
There were metallic stutterings in the grass.
I could not tell what made them
and I was far from home.

Farther than ever now in the new world,
I have listened to the stories of those
whose dreams always return them to the same place.
"I go home every night, I can find it in my sleep,"
they say as if it were easy.
My dreams take me to cramped, anonymous rooms,
where strangers whisper together.

Brigitte Frase

The first time I saw the Arizona desert,
I thought I was close
to the last place on earth.
Air and ground naked against one another,
the sky was no longer a conceptual roof
held up by the structures of men,
but a membrane, a worldskin,
alive as I was alive.
We flowed through one another.
Here I might lay down my green burdens
of memories, inscrutable loves,
the weight of double names, endless allegiances,
to shed in the singular blue
layer after layer,
the whole dim house of the self
and all the words I had thought
were keys or gateways.

I walked on sharp pebbles,
on sparse crackling grass.
The bleached rocks were impassive.
Is this how it is, coming home?
Not the labor of making connections,
it is simply
to be around, nothing kept back,
but offered casually
on the open palm.
I wandered idly and picked up a stone,
seamed and layered in many colors.
With one finger I followed the grain of the world.

Brigitte Frase

# Yuba City School

From the black trunk I shake out
my one American skirt, blue serge
that smells of mothballs. Again today
Neeraj came crying from school. All week
the teacher has made him sit
in the last row, next to the fat boy
who drools and mumbles,
picks at the spotted milk-blue
skin of his face, but knows
to pinch, sudden-sharp,
when she is not looking.

The books are full of black curves,
dots like the eggs the boll-weevil laid
each monsoon in the furniture-cracks
in Ludhiana. Far up in front
the teacher makes word-sounds
Neeraj does not know. They float
from her mouth-cave, he says,
in discs, each a different color.

Chitra Divakaruni

Candy-pink for the girls
in their lace dresses, matching
shiny shoes. Silk-yellow
for the boys beside them,
crisp blond hair, hands raised
in all the right answers,
who never look back. Behind them
the Mexicans, whose older brothers,
he tells me, carry knives,

whose catcalls and whizzing rubber bands
clash, mid-air, with her
voice, its sharp purple edge.
For him, the words are
a muddy red, flying low and heavy,
and always one he has learned to understand:
idiot, idiot, idiot.

I heat the iron over the stove. Outside
evening blurs the shivering
in the eucalyptus. Neeraj's shadow
disappears into the hold
he is hollowing all afternoon.
The earth, he knows, is round, and if
one can tunnel all the way through,
he will end up in Punjab,
in his grandfather's mango orchard,
his grandmother's songs
lighting on his head,
the old words glowing
like summer fireflies.

Chitra Divakaruni

In the playground, Neeraj says,
invisible hands snatch at his uncut hair,
unseen feet trip him from behind,
and when he turns, ghost laughter
all around his bleeding knees.
He bites down on his lip
to keep in the crying. They are
waiting for him to open his mouth,
so they can steal his voice.

I test the iron with little drops of water
that sizzle and die. Press down
on the wrinkled cloth. The room fills
with a smell like singed flesh.
Tomorrow in my blue skirt I will go
to see the teacher, my tongue
stiff and swollen
in my unwilling mouth, my few
English phrases. She will pluck them
from me, nail shut my lips. My son
will keep sitting in the last row
among the red words that drink his voice.

Chitra Divakaruni

# Invisibility Poem: Lesbian

There's quite enough to
identify her
should you have forgotten
her name:
That woman who lives in
who teaches
who speaks
who looks like
who writes about
the one who knows
the one who made
the one who loves to
who likes to wear
whose daughter
who used to be
wasn't she married to
didn't she once spend some time
Every known thing about her
is like a smell
reassuring, familiar
"She is like      us"
"We are like      her"
No need to watch
suspiciously
when she walks by.

Ilze Mueller

Not as familiar perhaps
the things she keeps
invisible:
The woman with whom
the circle of friends that she
the way she feels when
the thoughts she doesn't
the fear that keeps her from
the times she imagines
the price she pays for

Ilze Mueller

# Christmas in the Midwest

I brought a lover home
in midwest snow.
My parents said:
You sleep here, he there,
so we made love here
and there when the garage door slammed
and the house beat like a clock
around us. I dreamed

I was arrested
in a VW bug with the stickshift
hard against my leg
by the Cary police force, shining
high beams on my breasts. Why
does sex ignite authority?

My parents received word
of my defection to women
peaceably. They pretended not
to be surprised—
"the way the world is. . .
the way men are. . ."—
and said they'd treat her
kindly at Christmas
as they would any female friend.

Maureen Seaton

They made no mention
of "here and there." We slept
like children in a double bed
beneath handmade quilts,
trying heroically to stay afloat
without their disapproval, the headlights
of a straight society to validate us.

*Maureen Seaton*

# La Foto Que Mira

Yo, que tantos angeles he sido.

En la plaza se reúne la gente.
El silbo penetrativo
tiñe la pluma
cuando decir piedra es insulto.

En la ascensión abro mis brazos
y atrapo tus inevitables reflejos.
No lloro.
La paz avanza hacia nosotros,
se encierra en nuestra casa.

Los soldados me empujan.
Salgo del sueño.
Confieso que te conozco.
Desterrada, muero.

Tu sombra entra en mi cuerpo.
En la plaza se reúne la gente.
El silbo penetrativo
tiñe la pluma.

Acusada de herejáa me transformo.
Acusado de ángel te llevan.

Intuyo el abrazo.
Llega la entrega.

Tú, que tantos ángeles has sido.

Carlota Caulfield

# The Photo That Watches

*Translated by Carol Maier*

I, who have been so many angels.

In the square people gather.
The piercing hiss
tinges the pen
when the word stone insults.

During the ascent I open my arms
and catch your inevitable reflections.
I do not weep.
Peace comes toward us,
locks herself in our house.

Soldiers push me.
I emerge from the dream.
I confess that I know you.
Exiled, I die.

Your shadow enters my body.
In the square people gather.
The piercing hiss
tinges the pen.

Branded a heretic, I change form.
Branded an angel, you are taken.

I intuit the embrace.
Self's present is passed.

You, who have been so many angels.

*Carlota Caulfield*

# Grief

After the Ghanaian dancing, we fought
about monogamy, whether
to separate with it or without. Never
mind the impossibility
of sleeping near someone else's skin,
you said, you'd throw up! Well,
I could have watched them dance all
night, how could you
have fallen asleep? Once you snored,
and when I nudged you said: "I'm woke!"
Sure. Everyone around us clapping,
jerking in their seats, you
leaving for donuts during Sohu.
I loved the way their bright
asses monopolized the stage, those
drums like a thousand hungers. Maybe
you've heard them all your life,
maybe it's cliché to love the music
of your homeland. But no one else slept
at the finale, and when the medicine
woman, with the pot of herbs on her head
like the burden of a people, threw
holy water at the two of us,
maybe you didn't need the bath, but
I did. And I wonder: What does Africa
mean to a Black New Yorker? And why
did you hurt so hard you had to sleep?

Maureen Seaton

# the quickness of fear

putting away wedding gifts
your teacup
shatters      suddenly

I realize
I am waiting for you
to leave me

Beverly Acuff Momoi

# Portrait

*Watashi wa Bebari desu.*
*Dozo yoroshiku.*

Hair—shiny black geisha hair
Not hers
A wig, seven pounds heavy,
Keeping her chin down
Acquiescent.
Curious eyes poking up.

They dressed her.
Palest of petal pink under-kimono
Like the finest silk slip
Wrapped like a doll
Hands wrapping one layer over the next
Three layers of kimono
Or was it four?
Red and white outer-kimono
Red and white, the colors of celebration,
The colors of wedding.
They say the best silk is made in Kyoto,
Its colors dyed in the river that runs through the town
Red rushing tears the morning of its dyeing.
Obi waist, stiff green and gold,
Riot of color
Contained
Binding her to them.

Beverly Acuff Momoi

They whitened her face
Gentle hands painting her
Neck and hands
Sharp features thrown into relief
Against stark white.
Doe brown around her eyes
To draw them
Out and down
Attempts to un-round them.

Time for the family picture.
The bride seated
Front and center
Candle light framing her white face
Glancing off hazel eyes
Flecks of green and gold
Not black brown almond eyes
Like the others.
Lips—full red from the crush of flowers
Crimson stain made from the oils of
Hundreds of flowers.
The stain of history
Geishas use this to color their lips
Have for centuries.
Other women once in their life
Their wedding day.
Do flowers bleed?
Their blood on her lips.

Beverly Acuff Momoi

Ten years later, a friend,
Whose mother is Japanese,
Exclaimed over my picture.
"My God . . . except for the eyes
You could almost pass."
Almost
Pass for what?
Made in Japan
Almost
Me/yet not me.
Except for the eyes
And the language, of course.
I knew
No words then.
Swaddled in the sounds and sure hands of women
I could not speak
In their language
Now
You cannot shut me up.

My husband says,
"I do not want to bind you.
Be yourself."
Now
My legs move freely in
Great open strides
Remembering
Tiny bunched steps
Toes that grasped brocade thongs
One October day

Beverly Acuff Momoi

10 years ago.
Closed careful steps
Careful to keep the kimono
Tightly wrapped
Legs together.
Appearance is everything.

Now, she looks back at me.
Remember
Remember the first words
That were mine
Yet
Not mine.
Words he taught me
Before we met his parents.
When I look at the picture
And see her
The phrase comes back.

*Watashi wa Bebari desu.*
*Dozo yoroshiku.*
My name is Beverly.
Please be nice to me.

Beverly Acuff Momoi

# Sondra

You stock the shelves with quick-food—baked beans, canned peas, chips, mini-boxes of Kellogg's cornflakes imported for American tourists—standing on tiptoe to reach the top, pulling at the short red skirt which rides up your thigh. He bought it for you when he opened the store. Bring in more folks, he said.

Outside, bougainvilleas explode magenta against a December sky thick with ocean-smell and Christmas bells from St. James. All the other stores are closed today. More business for us, he said. You fluff out your frizzed hair and aim a bright bougainvillea smile at the small mirror on the wall by the cash register where Robbie and Nicky's photo is taped. You hope they're keeping out of trouble, out of their daddy's way, maybe mucking out the coops so you won't have to do it when you get home. You—he—owns a chicken farm and the brown eggs which you fondle, warm on the counter, are from birds you have named. Peggy, Linda, Suzie—and Gulabi, from a story your grandmother used to tell you. But you don't want to think about Gulabi because you fed her corn out of your palm, but then she stopped laying. And when you came home from the store he had already wrung her neck and you had to pluck her and cook her although you threw up in the sink twice. Pound her and cook her, because the meat was tough, and make her into kebabs to sell the next day.

Once your name was Sundari, meaning beautiful, and your parents' love wound tight and dark around you like the roots of the giant banyan growing over your house in Trinidad. But when they started writing home for bridegrooms, mailing your picture and horoscope back to India, you had to run. With a coal-skinned, casteless man, they said. They performed a purification ceremony

Chitra Divakaruni

and never mentioned you again, never replied to your letters from Barbados. Not when the first child came with its black crinkly hair, not when he left you for the lead limbo dancer at the Apple Experience, and you sick and throwing up with the other one who luckily died. Not when you had to work at the Roti Hut leaving Robbie with the landlady although you suspected she was giving him something in his sugarwater to keep him quiet while the smell of curry took your clothes and hair, and your skin stank of it no matter how much you scrubbed.

And then the white man with the cracked-eggshell eyes every day at the Roti Hut, watching you silently. When you got off work his rickety Volkswagen was so much better than sway-standing on the bus trying to push away the sweaty bodies pressing into you. Then his unmade bed with the sheets smelling faintly of chicken feathers and the crickets crying in the woodwork, his weight thrusting down, tearing in, his big man-hands gripping you after so, so long. The morning sickness started and you moved in, which was a good thing for both of you, because you cleaned up the place and cooked and did his laundry and saved him money and kept him from the drink at least some of the time. And he gave you a safe place to stay, an almost-home, a body to hold onto through the quicksand nights. He let the children call him daddy and was mostly kind and hardly ever took his belt to them as long as you all stayed out of his way when his white friends came around.

And now, the store with its creamy-clean shelves gleaming with multicolored cans, the little glass-topped counter stocked with your own kebabs and rotis. The freezer hidden in the back with the illegal beer that the workmen so love, coming in from the blazing midday calling you pretty lady, brown sugar, darlin', stroking you

Chitra Divakaruni

in your short red skirt with their hot eyes and letting you keep the
change if it isn't too much. And recently he's been saying if the
business keeps up, in three, maybe two years, he'll take you and
the kids to Florida, to Disneyworld. You know what's in
Disneyworld. The woman who owns the laundry service down on
Hastings Main Road went there last year. She's told you all about
them—Mickey and Minnie, the Singing Bears, the boat ride
through fire and water in the pirate's cave, the tallest, fastest
rollercoaster in the world which pulls your screaming stomach up
into your dusty mouth, the room filled with snowflakes where you
become tiny, tiny, tiny, until you disappear. You know them all,
and you say them to yourself in that high singsong voice that is for
Nicky's bedtime, as you caress the eggs, their frail brown skins,
with a bougainvillea finger, standing in the middle of the empty
shop waiting for customers while darkness drops around you
like a net.

Chitra Divakaruni

126

# Nochebuena

Where I come from we have no snow
or winter solstice or sleigh rides.
There are no fireplaces to roast
chestnuts at nights.

We have the sun all around,
a sun that shines immediately
after those heavy rains when trees fall
and people from the slums drown.

After the deaths, always the sun—
not giving families the right
to have a gray day to mourn.
I remember funerals on sunny days
and Christmas Eves
where children, barefoot,
played with water.
Christmas Eve
*Nochebuena*: The good night.

I have forgotten the Christmas carols
that I memorized as a child
and cannot follow my daughter's voice
when she sings in a language
that I learned alone in an apartment
with a dictionary, the newspaper,
and the television always on.

Rosario Caicedo

And now after Halloween and Thanksgiving,
my children's Christmas comes.
Their laughter is heard in this big house
that in December has a decorated tree
and painted snowflakes on the walls.
They say that Santa Claus is coming.

Sometimes I feel
that I've been left
with nothing.

Rosario Caicedo

# Remembering Mexico, 1969

*for Nancy*

We were dauntless then.
We deadended on dirt roads
and called it *suerte*, luck.
Slept in corn fields under stars
thick as spilt salt; washed our hair
on the balcony in the rain; ate *tortas*
and mangos from street vendors and
fell in love with strangers
whose names we could barely pronounce.

Now you are an attorney
and spend your days in linen suits.
And I am teaching in a town
known only for its soybeans.
Sometimes on the highway

I turn my headlights to dim
then dare myself to plunge into
the thick wall six feet ahead.
And for a moment I remember
how it feels
to be succored
on the edge
of danger.

Barbara Lau

# New York City Mira Mira Blues

From the freeway you can almost
hear them screaming in their
red brick coops
      HELP ME, HELP ME
through glass grids silhouetted
like chicken wire against the
skyscrapers of Madison, Fifth,
Park, and lately Third Avenue,
where the old el used to shield
the homeless, now homes the shielded.
O Marcantonio! What did you do
to this city in your urgent need
to sprinkle liberalism like holy
water on the heads of the oppressors?
You should have played fair, *hombre*:
you should have left the *jíbaros*
in the mountains of their *Isla Bonita*,
perched like birds of paradise
on Cerro Maravillas observing
the rise and fall of the earth's curve
as it slumbers beneath the sea;
left them in El Fanguito, squatting
on squatters squatting on the land
that once was theirs; left them
in Borinquen, where there was no cool
assessment of who owned what,
no color line splitting families
in two or three, where everyone,
*todo el mundo*, was tainted
with *la mancha de plátano*—but no,
you needed votes. Sure votes.

Gloria Vando

Had to buy them, fly them in by
planeloads, skies darkening thickly
with visions of *barrios* to come.
Since it was so easy getting in, you'd
think it would be easy getting out, but
where to go, and who'll take you in?
Take you in, yes; but give you shelter?

The Triborough Bridge, 50 years old
in gold cloth 50 feet high spanning
its towers, waves greetings to us as
we cross the East River, where I swam
as a child, running home as fast as
I could to stash my sopping clothes
in the hamper before Abuelita found
out and exiled me to my island bed.
Now dressed in punk colors, FDR Drive
shouts SAVE EARTH: GIVE A SHIT and
raises a SHAKER-KLASS-AMERICA fist
to the inmates on Welfare Island
whose view of the newyorkcityskyline
is optimum, while the rich on Sutton
Place and York only get to see slums.
Welfare Island whose one aesthetic
function is to spew enough smoke and
soot into the air to obscure Queens
and itself, if the wind is right,
in a merciful eclipse. Welfare Island,
where poet Julia de Burgos was confined,
forgotten, all her protest silenced
with yet another 2 c.c.s of thorazine.

*Gloria Vando*

On 110th Street, my concrete manger
overlooking Central Park, only Spanish
signs remain to remind us of the second-
to-the-last immigration wave: Cubanos
seeking refuge when corruption takes
a backseat to red slogans, red tape.
The Bay of Pigs non-invasion spurs
them on to invade us, Miami first, then
slowly up the coast like a spreading
thrombosis that ruptures in Nueva York,
where all Hispanics blend into one
faceless thug, one nameless spic.

The cab cuts like a switchblade
across the park; I try to hear Ives'
marching bands meeting in noisy combat
on Sheeps Meadow, but later sounds
intrude, reintroduce themselves
like forgotten kin—midnight, a baby
carriage, my mother crossing the park
from her sitter's on the Eastside
to her husband's on the West. And she,
loving the leaves' black dance against
the night, recalls her mother's warning
that she not try to blot out the sky
with one hand, but oh! there beneath
the trees, the immensity of space is
palpable—she feels safe. And lacing

Gloria Vando

the earth, a fragrance she cannot discern
causes her to yearn for home. She hums

half expecting the *coquis* to sing along.
It is that time of night when muggers
are out—even then before the word
was out—blending into shadows, bushes,
trees, like preview footage of Vietnam,
waiting to assault whatever moves,
whatever breathes. She breathes hard
but moves so fast they cannot keep up.
Westside Story before they learned
that death set to music could make
a killing at the boxoffice. With one
Robbins-like leap up a steep incline,
we escape; I sleep through it. Now
I'm wide awake watching every leaf quake
in the wind as her young limbs in flight
must have then, fifty years ago
on that moonless night in Central Park
where fifty years before that
sheep grazed and innocence prevailed.

*Gloria Vando*

We exit on 86th Street, head down
Central Park West, past the Dakota
to our safe harbor in the heart
of Culture and Good Manners with
Lincoln Center only steps away.
Next door a flop house. Old people
with swollen legs sunning themselves
on folding chairs, used shopping
bags with someone's trash,
their treasure, at their feet.
The buzzards of the human race
cleaning up other people's droppings.
We walk around them, as though
proximity could contaminate. Nearby
those less prosperous prop themselves
up against their own destruction.

I see my children stepping carefully
between them, handing out coins
like Henry Ford. I see them losing
faith, losing hope, losing ground.
But I am *home*, I tell myself.
Home from the wheat and the corn
of Middle America, where whole-
someness grows so tall you cannot
see the poverty around you, grows
so dense the hunger cannot touch you.
Home to the familiar, the past; my
high school moved comfortably closer,
renamed LaGuardia for the Little Flower

*Gloria Vando*

who captured our hearts with *Pow!*
*Wham!* and *Shazam!* on newsless
Sunday mornings during the war.
Home to my Westside condo with free
delivery from columns A to Z,
a xenophobic's dream come true.
Home to the city's long shadows
casting tiers up, across, and down
skyless streets and buildings,
an Escher paradox turning a simple
journey to the corner into a fantasy
in chiaroscuro. Yes, I'm home.
Home, where my grandmother's aura
settles softly and white like
a shroud of down, stilling, if only
for a moment, the island's screams.

———

Definitions for those who might need them.

*mira*: look; also used as an exclamation to call attention, like "hey!"
*jíbaro*: hill-billy, peasant, now a national symbol
*Isla Bonita*: pretty island (refers to Puerto Rico)
*El Fanquito*: San Juan squatters' slums
*todo el mundo*: everybody
*mancha de plátano*: stain from viscous secretions of the plaintain;
    refers to the native P.R.
*Abuelita*: little grandmother
*coqui*: tree frog indigenous only to Puerto Rico; it cannot survive
    elsewhere
music: beginning of the popular song "Puerto Rico"

———

*Gloria Vando*

# The Administrator

The women are within her, smoking angel dust, sipping tea,
when, suddenly, he enters with his chest bare. He
from the other world of slender black ties and shiny shoes—
the keeper of the gate, the purveyor of keys. He says,
"You would not bite the hand that feeds you, Diana." And so,
she succumbs to him . . . and those within chant the song of the
    prairie:
the beast does what beasts do as the lion plays with his maw,
and the carrion teases the condor. In the morning, he walks
down the dim corridor and greets her, as always, in his
official tone, high and horselike. "Good morning, Diana,
did you have a good sleep?" And she ponders on the meaning
of sleep—A skeleton pushing a gondola across the water. When
will she reach the other side? Will there be lions in wait?
Pills to swallow? Papers to sign? From across his large white desk
he opens his leather-bound files. Again, again chant the witnesses,
"The state is your conservator; the prairie will be your life!"

Marilyn Chin

# Night Shift at the Fruit Cannery

The thin neon light spills on the hands in the tubs,
the pale halves of the pears that must be dipped in salt water to
keep from turning brown,
the endless procession of cans that moves past the women
now and at midnight and dawn and on and on
even in sleep, even in dream.
Fingers turn wrinkled, turn pale like the pears,
take on a life of their own as they nestle the slippery fruit
spoonfashion in the can,
barely stopping to push the straggling hair back under the scarf.
No time to talk, no time to look up,
nothing to look up at.
Time has stopped, there is no yesterday, no tomorrow, no moment
but now, no place but here,
this slave ship hurtling through eons of empty space.
And at the whistle which rends the rumble and clatter and din that
taught their ears not to hear,
the women stumble outside like children woken too early for
school,
stretching stiff limbs and creaking necks, testing a voice rusty from
lack of use.
Still dazzle-eyed, they look up and see
stars in their multitudes blazing over their heads.

Ilze Mueller

# Where We Are

Bertha let me run barefoot those weeks
at her house. I learned Bible verses
and picked red-stem peppermint from cow creeks
for the tea she steeped in milk jugs.
Thor stem we hung to dry in the attic
for Grandpa's stomach. She called flies
the Mister and Misses we mustn't let in
through the breezeway where fleisig Lizzies
bloomed in the windows. In the cellar
she peeled peaches while steam clattered the lid
of a speckled canner and I scampered
behind her: Three guesses, where am I?
And she'd guess, Under the steps? Behind
the jam closet? Back of the box of cans
Daddy should dump off the mountain side soon?
But I'd be in the dark root cellar, crouched
with sprouting potatoes under shelves of pickles,
green and wax beans, red, white, and sour cherries,
and the horrible beef canned in its tallow.
Three guesses, where am I? Her letters still find me
On paper printed with birds and Bible verses
she writes, Greetings in Jesus' name.
Come for a weekend, a week. And we must thank God
you will not stay in that city forever.
Instead, I thank God I can still find her
poking her pots of African violets or bent
over the counter, crimping the crust on a pie.
She's still there in that silence, bowing her head
before meals, breathing desirous prayers
or remembering how she flew home to us,

Julia Kasdorf

grandpa's corpse hidden deep in the plane,
how from take-off to landing, she stitched
garlands of daisies on quilt blocks,
her needle tacking black knots on the blooms,
so where ever I use this quilt,
I'll see those seeds and think of grandpa.
Yet it's her I see, hunched in the soft spot
of airplane light, embroidering above him, alive.

Julia Kasdorf

# The Parachutist's Wife

Six men turned to smoke in the next square
of air, their plane became wind.
You were twenty-three. Hands over your ears, a roaring
in your veins, a silence
on the radio.
        Flak
knocked twice at the cockpit,
dull knuckles, thumping:
Let me in,
      let me in.

You knew you had to
give yourself to the sky the way we
give ourselves to music—no knowing
the end of the next bar, no figuring
how the chord will fall.

The clouds were cold, the plane trembled.
You pulled the cord and the chute
"bloomed like God's love," a heavenly
jockstrap anchoring you in air.

You were happy, you say, you were
never happier than that day, falling
into birth: the archaic
blue-green map of Europe glowed below you.

Sandra M. Gilbert

You were going to camp, you were
going to be free of death.
The pull of the harness, the swaying,
the ropes creaking—it was so peaceful up there,

like a page of Greek or
an afternoon in a Zen monastery
or a long slow stroll around
somebody's grandfather's garden.

I'm quiet in my kitchen, I won't
bail out, I don't think it would be the same
for me, I think if I
fell like that the hands of flak
would strip me as I
swung from the finger of God, I'd

offer myself as a bright idea
and a chorus of guns
would stammer holes in my story, nothing

would lift me over the black fangs
of the Alps, I'd dangle
like bait and the savage

map of Europe would eat me up.
I stick like grease to my oven, I wear
a necklace of dust,

my feet root in green stone.
You've forgotten I'm here!
But every morning

Sandra M. Gilbert

there are crystals of ice in my hair
and a winter distance glitters
in the centers of my eyes.

I don't need to stroll through the sky
like a hero:
in my bone cave

I marry the wind.

Sandra M. Gilbert

# Pillar of Flame

A clumsy cross burns
on my grandfather's lawn
in Woodside, Queens,
smoke seen as far as Manhattan.

The Holocaust is still years away.

Moving as in a dream, you take your place
in the crowd beside your grandmother,
children hiding behind her apron.

The eldest, your mother, stands apart
in her great unmoved scorn.
Together they watch the flames.

Your grandfather arrives, natty in spats,
gloves and cane, sees your mother
accuse him with eyes like targets.
He, who wanted his children to cross the border
denied by birth to him,
who brought them to this
pillar of flame.

But a man must stand and fight,
not run like a coward,
as trembling rookies will learn years later
or women as the soldiers enter the village.

Barbara Unger

Now your mother touches you lightly
out of the grave.
A comfortless rain
washes over it
as neighbors guard their eyes
from pity or blame.

Now when American lamps dim
and the bully kings swashbuckle
in a drunken rage writing a script
of hate in an alphabet of flame,
I recognize the stench.
I can set the sky behind it.

Barbara Unger

# First Lessons

It is not the hunter who is cunning
but the hunted who has learned
to dash into that familiar hole
until the dogs pass.

It is not the gun cocked
or the fingers caressing the trigger
that makes us march
somnambulantly on.

There is no guiding light from heaven,
for I can hear the blind ox
tapping her foot in the darkness
to find the path.

It is not the pottage but the cauldron
that is our enchantment—
mother's flesh and father's dictum
our succor. And Diana,

the eyes between her ancestors and the world—
was studying to become a citizen
in early August ember.
And I, her unworthy tutor

failed to tell her about the fifty paltry stars
that amount to a little more
than sensible graphics
and fine accounting.

Marilyn Chin

And despite my tutelage
somebody had drafted her purpose,
stamped "destination: elsewhere,"
and "re-entry denied."

My last glimpse of her
was a bad, impish drawing
pinned—a hollow specimen—
flapping on the wall.

And what will be remembered
of that summer lesson
but a moth dying on the screen,
leaving her face-powder.

Marilyn Chin

# Russia 1914/Bolinas 1988

Out of my window high as aerie
I can see the ocean.
The birds caw madly in the eucalyptus.
Later. I walk the beach collecting
soft crab shells, branched coral,
purple kelp, the half exposed skull
                                    of a bird.
I pile this slough into plastic bags.
The stink of their bodies colors
the air.

Far away in another land,
                my grandmother sleeps.
In her dream, she is wounded by
Cossacks, their greasy coats smelling
                        of sheep and blood.
These men with coarse hands    whet
their knives on her doorframe.
My grandmother's throat is tender,
her flesh,
        soft as white flour.
Outside there is snow, it is snowing,
the house will be buried in snow.

*Gail Shafarman*

My grandmother never wakes
                    from this dream.
She never sees her granddaughter
                    waiting for her
by the lip of the ocean.
Never takes her granddaughter's hand.
Never touches her fingers,
                    ripe with the odor
of salt, of fish, of water,
of blood.

Gail Shafarman

# Exmatriate

I. Nightmères

waking to drizzle and the inevitable
egg   dream fragments drying
on the rims of my eyes
why am I always taking trains
across the ocean   rushing for planes
on a forged ticket   caught
with a bomb in my bag?
in dreams I am never ready,
never on time   frantically I tie
a blue kimono round my nakedness
while mother   unperturbed
says *don't worry, I'll drive you*

it's like that every night:
I'm back, I pack, I try
to leave the mother country

oh mama, missed my
connection.


II. Mère Méditerranée

three years on an island, lotus-
eater, languishing, in love
with sunlight, writing
to mother of motherly women,
mother-in-law, grandmothers
drying like raisins on their doorsills

Jacqueline Lapidus

149

when she arrives
armed with guidebook and bathing suit
I am already a stranger,
speaking an ancient language with my hands
she confers grandma's diamond
on my finger,
finds my house bare   my womb
has just been scraped dry
sullen, we stumble through the beehive tomb
clutching our husbands

                         secrets

                                    lies


III. *Notre Dame de Paris*

spider in the interstice between
two lives, I have survived
a coup d'état
domestic servitude
postal strikes
partouzes
I have cracked the Napoleonic Code
I emerge, blinking, from organ pipes
to find I missed the 60s
and the war
I am spinning a web of my own
attracting visitors like flies
some day it might be turned into a novel:
*the first ten years were the hardest*

———

Jacqueline Lapidus

now my accent is nondescript
as a passport, this fabled city
just another one-horse town
where I am teaching   again
the alchemy of words
home
is where my books are
I leave the hustle for cheap flights
free phones   to those
who just got off the boat
my papers are in order
my number listed
my line: busy


IV. *Some People Consider This a Safe Position*

wondering how long   waiting
for a sign   the fifth gold inlay
the first grey hair
a gap in family snapshots where
        the piano used to be
a death

Jacqueline Lapidus

*V. Mother/Right*

high above the Seine, bewildered
in this roomful of happy women
she cannot tell the mothers
from the daughters
something
about the way they kiss
upon parting, *what's*
*going on here?*

> a swarm of bees
> a school of fish
> a flight of swans
> a flock of ewes
> a gaggle of geese
> a herd of cows
> a pride of lionesses

explaining in letters: here
my past is past, I melt
into crowds unrecognized,
vault over barriers I do not even see
here where the rooted fail
to bother me, I find room
to listen to voices in my head
and strength for the women in my arms

Jacqueline Lapidus

my pleasure
grows in correspondence
dear mother,
this ocean wide and salt enough
nourishes us both
and it was you who taught me
how to swim
        I've gone back
the way you came,
singing my mother-tongue
eating dry bread in steerage
for a glimpse of the new world

Jacqueline Lapidus

# My Mother's Homeland

Translated by Pamela Carmell

My mother always said
your homeland is any place,
preferably the place where you die.
That's why she bought the most arid land,
the saddest landscape,
the driest grass,
and beside the wretched tree
began to build her homeland.
She built it by fits and starts
     (one day this wall, another day the roof;
from time to time, holes to let air squeeze in).
My house, she would say, is my homeland,
and I would see her close her eyes
like a young girl full of dreams
while she chose, once again, groping,
the place where she would die.

Belkis Cuza Malé

# Mother

I wish that I could talk with her again.
That's what I thought of when I thought of home,
Always supposing I had a home to come to.
If she were here, we'd warm the Chinese pot
To brew a jasmine-scented elixir,
And I would tell her how my life has been—
All the parts that don't make sense to me,
And she would let me talk until the parts
Fitted together.

That will never be.
She couldn't wait for me to come to her—
Ten years away. I couldn't wish for her
To wait, all blind and helpless as she was.
So now I have come home to emptiness:
No silly welcome-rhyme, no happy tears,
No eager questioning. No way to get
An answer to my questions. Silence fills
The rooms that once were vibrant with her song,
And all the things I wanted to talk out
With her are locked forever in my heart.

I wander through the rooms where she is not.
Alone I sit on the hassock by her chair,
And there, at last, I seem to hear her voice:
"You're a big girl now. You can work things out."

*Bea Liu*

155

# FOUR

"Not sure of weather or welcome . . ."

—Marilyn Boe
"Sunday Afternoon at the State Hospital"

# Sunday Afternoon at the State Hospital

I've come to see a stranger
wearing my daughter's face,
living a life I never knew.
Her eyes, heavy with drugs or disinterest
look down at her feet or stare
at a shadow behind me.

We go to the Canteen for a Coke,
a cup of coffee,
the sort of offer I make
when I'm helpless and need to fold
my hands around an object
warm and familiar, almost a living shape.

I am the odd one,
in from the snow outside,
unable to understand the jokes,
teasing I hear between patients,
and I know nothing about anyone
in this room, not even my own,
our communication severed
like a slashed wrist.

Not sure of weather or welcome,
my hands hold the chill of both,
made worse by TV's warnings;
glare ice and guesswork on roads
on the way back.

Marilyn Boe

I need to find friendly landmarks
inside the swirling snow;
Southdale Center or Cal's Tree Lot,
to guide me, so I won't stay lost
in the dark mystery of my daughter's face.

Marilyn Boe

# Oradour-sur-Glane. Silence.

April. I have wheeled you to the park
beside the hospital. You are quiet, taking in the landscape
like another world. Last week you wept at the fierce green
of the grass and the young leaves that seemed to fly
through the late afternoon sun. You sit
                                        more firmly
in your chair than yesterday. Today your face
is dry. You study the objects around you as though, home
after a long absence, you are counting up
changes. Sometimes you gaze intently, at what
I cannot tell, then blink and fasten hard on another
direction, as though trying to remember, as though you do not
recognize
            anything. I break you a spray of lilac
and you sniff it carefully as though you are lost.
                                        I am lost
in an exhaustion of memories too new to sort, too sharp to trust
them in my mouth, they will saw out my teeth. Silence
comes down hard on us, except I can think into words:
     *you are not dying anymore*
and now the word *death* falls easy as grace
on my tongue though I cannot say it to you. You sit still
as death, your needle-ravaged arms locked around your lap
like a bruised wall holding something in. I want you
                                        to speak,
want to speak to you, want to feel the din of your paralyzed
utterance fill my head again, rapid-fire alphabet on my tongue
making your words, making you, quicken
                              even the air with your
                                        living

Lucia Cordell Getsi

needs. I do not want this. It is too much the silence
of ruins, of cold spots in hauntings that mark where violence
happened, or memorials

                        like Oradour


        after the Nazis. We entered the ruined French village
through walls hung with irrelevant signs: *Silence*. No one,
not even birds, made a noise in all that verdant green
around bare footings of houses, trees thick and incongruous
in the remains

                        of town buildings. No living creature moved,
not even one bird cried, though all France is a garden
for birds, no one sleeps past the morning chatter.

                                                Late afternoon
the S.S. marched through Oradour to break down
resistance. They met none, everyone home from fields and work.
Easy to call them outside, coatless against their surprise
(*it is the other Oradour, surely, on another river, surely no
resistance here*),

                        easy to drive women and children into the church,
encircle the men on the square and gun them into the grass, throw
the bodies down the well, firebomb the church

                                        where women

                                                        listened
trapped, clutching children. One scaled the high wall above
the Stations of the cross to a window, hauling her child
on her back, and escaped, leaping to the woods. One, late
in coming home, stayed safe in the border of trees. A man, living,
crawled up out of the well. That is all

                        who speak a witness


                                        ⸻

                                        *Lucia Cordell Getsi*

into the silent rows of family names buried
in the central mausoleum. The bodies remain where they fell,
sealed inside the church, in the well.

        There are no traces
of violence. Only here and there the bare jutting
of a wall, outlines of rooms like blueprints, the rusted
skeleton of a car or an iron bed. Edging the footings, grass
grows like an assault.

      We did not speak, though horror dropped
through us like stones, and something like tears kept wanting to rise
past them, breaking over the heavy quiet like tidewater.

                Like now.


  I want to come to you, to hold you against some inward
breaking. I have held you so long against the clamor
of not letting you die, the clank of instruments, the whoosh
and buzz of life-support equipment, held you inside the screams
of ambulances, beyond the clutch

         of phones ringing at night,
the conferring whispers of doctors, held you high above dreams
of snapping death jaws, the intense beeping of red alert
signals in a body shriven by fear—

           this silence stops me.
You sit buried in yourself, all your names
for this locked up, leaping to your tense eyes that shock
me like Chagall's blue windows, breaking

            your nails to climb out,

               clawing

your way past dead bodies in a well.


Lucia Cordell Getsi

# Exiles

My father beat the robins
From his maple
Swinging an old piece of lath
Before any babies came.
"Damn noisy mess," he muttered
Raking the nest from its fragile branch
Three spring mornings in a row.

Birds scattered, he turned to me.
Too soon I packed
Skates and school geography maps
And set out like the birds
For Florida, which I had colored
The warm dark green of our old Packard sedan,
And never brought my babies home.

judy f. ham

# Case Study:

*Abuse, but the girl's*
*room clean, adequate. Father*
*and stepmother say they care*
*but have no space, except*
*the basement. Mother will take*
*child but only if custody*
*reassigned first, a matter*
*of months...*

Meanwhile, the child regresses
from seven to a diapered three,
too timid to speak in school, in court,
too frightened to ask for a room
upstairs, away from spiders who live
in the basement, cool and dark—
an adequate home for arachnids
and little girls.

There, common house spiders, comb-
footed spiders, dance
all night on her pillow, drop
from the ceiling onto soft
eyelids, whisper secrets to her inner
ear. She wakes to these tangled
web-weavers hanging from drag
lines, their segmented bodies lit
by the moon caught in the window well.
And the girl cowers under quilts,
her eyes tracking the slight shadows
as they circle the walls of her room
and bank at sharp angles near the ceiling.

Gayle Kaune

The spiders want only to be close,
their eight shiny legs always scurrying
near. All night while she jerks
in her dreams, their silk nets
connect bed to wall, drape
the rungs of her chair, vibrate
with their eager feet.

*Gayle Kaune*

# IV. For My Mother, Who Lives

We come from a long line
of ancestors who didn't survive,
thought suicide more satisfying
than miserable lives
that threatened their destinies.
Dedicek waited till eighty-five,
put the knife to his throat.
When angina didn't improve,
Uncle Tony took the noose.

Cather's Mr. Shimerda, another
pioneer Bohemian deprived
of violins in the concert hall,
saw one other avenue, like
many refined, cultured folk
defying life on the surface
the only way they knew. Too
used to beauty, legacy of books,
music, fine architectural lines,
the golden, ancient city
of Mozart, home of oldest
universities, Don Giovanni's
debut, despite long reigns
of oppressive rule,

Lorraine Duggin

how could they live now,
crude peasants, where soil
blew away like a house
of sand with the first gust
of wind, where ships filled
with immigrants spilled
onto prairie seas of wild
Nebraska grass without rock
for anchor, without roots?

Even today my daughter
studies accounts in the news,
numerous teen-age suicides.
Hopeless kids, sick with addiction,
no sense of family, nation,
pride, says she can sympathize.
In school they read "Paul's Case,"
see him a hero, identify,
believe his dying justified.

I wonder at sins of the fathers,
heritage, history we pass on,
remember Mother's veiled asides,
defeated sighs, Dad's revolver
in her bedside dresser drawer
atop a pile of crocheted
handkerchiefs she'd made,
my brother's illness at one
of its heights of violent pain.

Lorraine Duggin

I remember coming into the bedroom
late at night, terrified, my
brother's cries momentarily
subsiding. I'd lie silently
on the rose-edged pillowcase,
my body a living blockade
separating them from the drawer,
the gun inside, trying to remind
my mother of one thing I knew
with a child's quiet certainty,
making sure, too, she wouldn't

reach a despairing hand across me,
not that night, anyway.

Lorraine Duggin

# Handful of Pebbles, Mouthful of Stones

i

"So serious. Why don't you smile?"
my mother asks.

ii

Daddy gobbles my achievements like snacks.
I keep his cupboards full.
Upstairs he walks naked
and when I say to stop
he emerges pouting from the bath,
briefs held over genitals like a flag.
Before and after bottom slaps hello,
I see his eyes upon me feeding, shining,
see myself the centerpiece.

iii

Mother, depressed, is far from home.

*Pegatha Hughes*

iv

Twice married, I—
father first, then husband.
This one hurls oaths like bowling balls
at our children standing white and mute.
It isn't his fault they're loud
or leave their room a mess.
Charging through, he belts a bed,
just misses quivering feet.

Inside a dishrag,
outside a washcloth rinsed and wrung,
I sit with them til sleep can come.


v

Finally, I leave that place.

Pegatha Hughes

# Anticipation

The early sounding of one or more tones of a succeeding chord
to form a temporary dissonance.

—*Webster's New Collegiate Dictionary*


There is a grape vine threatening my house. It's taken over the backyard.
It killed the lilac bushes and the weight may pull the phone lines down.

My friend says the vines are prized for making baskets. She
suggests that I put an ad in the paper: "Free grape vines." People
would flock to my yard in droves, she says.

Every year when I take the Greyhound to Duluth to visit my sister,
I worry about being trapped in the chemical toilet.

My home is my castle, the vines my moat. I used to take
Norpramin© at 11 and wake up screaming at 3. The car was going
over a cliff. My father was driving, and I lay across the back seat. I
don't take antidepressants any more. They say the time you don't
wake up is the time you die.

I've given up driving. Once a month my folks drive me to
Rainbow Foods. We take the High Bridge, 100 feet above the
Mississippi River. I sit in the back.

Candy used to be my friend, until she told me that the hallmark of
good citizenship is returning library books on time. I got a card
from her at Christmas with a U.S. flag stamp.

A pair of cardinals nested in the back yard every spring and ate the
red berries that grew there.


Sheila Richter

The males in my family are the smart ones, the females, the clinging vines. Dad spent three and a half years in the Philippines during the War. He learned to say, "Are the bananas ripe yet?" in Tagalog, and when it was time to come home, he sent a telegram. Mother asked Uncle Al to balance her checkbook, unheeded all those months.

Candy told me, too, that not balancing your checkbook is like steering a car from the back seat. How did she know about my checkbook? How did she know about my dream?

And when Dad came home from a sales trip, he cursed Mother because she was menstruating.

Our house sat high on a hill. The surrounding streets were dead ends, and the police wandered, lost, the night there was a Peeping Tom.

Dad traveled to countries where he didn't speak the language, but he always found his way home.

*There is a grape vine threatening my house. It's taken over the back yard.*
*It killed the lilac bushes and the weight may pull the phone lines down.*

Sheila Richter

# Alien

They can enter the window and they will—
Martians from the void beyond
the safety of her childhood circle.

They wait in the blackness
behind the light reflected on the windowpane.

Their voices scratch the screen.

Their faces shift in and out of being
in the marble pattern
of the bathroom tile.
Pointy noses, empty eye sockets

leer back at her
from her own alien eyes
in the darkened mirror,

knowing her.
In the space behind her eyelids
their bones and rotting skulls
swell and shrink.

Their undulating flesh
grows and dies all at once,
as does she, this child afraid
of her own life.

Grows and dies
as does all else
in this vulnerable world

that wobbles daily into darkness,
into light.

Nancy Paddock

# A Single Space

The first nights alone, after my husband moved out and the kids took their turn at his house, I was alone, for the first time in my life, unless you count the loneliness of an unraveling marriage. I stayed in our house, an old Victorian three-story, not a house to wrap around you, but a procession of dignified rooms strung out like time, a family house, but the family had fled, and time cracked open.

I thought of myself as a statue, solitary and impassive, no longer surprised at anything. I saw myself as the figurehead of a ship, the kind my husband and I had seen years earlier in a museum in Boston harbor. During the day, as I went about the frantic task of reorganizing everything from my soul to my closet, the image of the woman, braced against wind came to me often.

Nights were worse. I reorganized the bedroom, buying an old bookcase headboard and mattress from a neighbor for $25. I lined up the books that I loved above my head. These seemed a kind of lifejacket I put on before I entered sleep.

Turning out the light, I curled up in the corner, the way an infant finds a place to curl in a crib. I seemed to split in two then, one part of me heavy, exhausted, welcoming the oblivion of sleep; the other, the figurehead, rising above the bed, the roof of the house, the city, the country, to consider my position in the world. What spatial claim was mine, now that I was just one person occupying a single space in a double bed? Was I held in God's eye or no eye at all?

I was so close to the child I was at seven, writing on paper in a small script, 296 Thomas Avenue, St. Paul, Minnesota, U.S. of A., Western Hemisphere, Earth, the Universe. It was months before the map of the universe with its locus in my bed faded; or the image of the woman floating out to sea.

Norita Dittberner-Jax

# Farewell

I search
for the straight path
back to wind
that only enters
through tall grass
as if none of it happened—
woman's crazed forehead brought to a floor,
a child damming tears behind stalwart eyes,
a million words pinioned in one man's brain—

We will hide there
in that tall grass
inside the wind.

I am taking with me
the entire blameless world:
All the children, trees and rivers, motley cats.
Single file, still as thieves,
we pass you now.

See, their hands are your
forgotten soft gods,
their faces the shy moons
of your childhood,
each lost essential silence.

How we love you!

But we are leaving.

Florence Dacey

# Super-Brave

my son's father is Kiowa-Comanche
at age three my son knows
that makes him Indian
he knows I am something different
I do not sing an opening song
beating against my boot
I do not carry him on shoulders
six feet high nor does my hair
shed water like a feather
he has not seen his father for two years
but at age three he knows
he needs something other than mother

he studies strong men who vanish
leading with a fist
he imitates gestures
of sudden transformation
pulling at small white buttons
to get his shirt open fast enough
to become Super-Brave   he wants
to find that phone booth   to see father
feathers sprouting in hair   he rips
at the edges where his shirt meets
over a child's bare chest

Teresa Whitman

at age three my son already knows
that red-and-blue is the color of alter-ego
that a single curl on the brow is not
the same as bangs slicked to the right
that he must fear the locomotive
at bedtime he wraps himself in a cape
pinned around the breath in his throat
he wants to be ready to fly high to see
what can only be seen with eyes like binoculars
the muscle and pitch of landscape
the wingbone of a man's shoulder

*Teresa Whitman*

# The Leaving

Who would have guessed she didn't have everything—
best house in town, lawn courts in back?

Her brother, the tennis twin, still let her win
and once on a dare she outran the freight to the slough.

With her father on back roads, she sat at the wheel
while he buried the dead, bought up farms

for back taxes. With her mother retiring and
her brother thought dull, she was prize Kuchen.

The world's wealth mailed to her, oranges and oysters.

—

Directions said nine months to master the instrument
but she wouldn't practice scales or one-person duets.

The piano just sat there, made the floor sag.
Much later in summers, her own child banged chords.

By then she was canning, red jelly in jars.
Her mother had died. She was queen of the realm.

Hot nights on the porch, her hair tugged the elms.
If she had any sorrow, only doves heard.

Brisk single walker, she was often alone,
except once, still early, her daughter yanked after her.

When church bells stopped ringing, she was beating the girl.
Whatever had caused it, she was simply too proud,

Margot Fortunato

couldn't stand her child's antics, up with the birds,
wouldn't take cast-offs from the sister-in-law's girls

The family was hers, and she couldn't bear sharing.
From the moment she left, her father condemned her.

Let the sister-in-law feed him. Gave her name to a bird.

—

Afterwards, did she ever come back? Wet the walk with her
tears? Once after rain, she paused by the Hardware,

gold H in her hair. By then her brother owned everything.
She built a house far away.

She could have used a fridge or a stove,
but he offered disposal. She had it put in.

Who knows if it worked? Remember,
things broke when they were first made?

This was an early one, worth just
what it cost her: nothing, disposed of.

No one saw her afterwards.

Margot Fortunato

# The Search

for my aunt, Margaret Stanek, who was admitted to a Minnesota state hospital
with a diagnosis of schizophrenia in 1938, died in the hospital on April 27,
1954. On April 27, 1989, I planted forget-me-nots on her grave.


1

Mugsy, what happened to you?
From all evidence,
you didn't exist
even when you were alive.
I sift through relative dates,
records that are burned,
memory banks that are empty.
I hear whispers:
locked in a closet, went crazy,
husband had a hatchet to keep her family at bay,
don't tell the sons.
I find a photograph of you, a flapper,
dark, wavy hair and dark eyes,
and a later photograph,
eyes downcast,
two beautiful sons at your heels.

I know so little about your family—
Gramma Kunugunda, a teenager aboard ship from Poland,
money stolen, property lost.
Later, only stay-at-home clothes for her and Grandpa.
Work in the garden and fishing the river
their only connection to this country.
She burned her wedding pictures, threw away her ring.
He refused to work after the operation,
sent the kids out at 13, their dreams
of nursing school left on the assembly line.

Nancy Peterson

These facts tell me the full extent of my inheritance—
the coat of not belonging.
But these stories don't hold me.
I'm drawn only to the unanswered questions.
Their memory loss
my driving force.


2

I ask the priests, were men sanctimonious
in their drinking, blessed to
rule the home? Were women good
only to have children, blessed to be silent
and obedient to men?

I ask the doctors, what was schizophrenia
for women in 1938? A label
for a battered wife? How does the body
react to terror? Can a whole family be
numbed by shock?

I ask Aunt Franny and my mom, Julia,
what was she like? How did you
give her over? Could no one stop the raising
of the arm? Would you
rather I create my own story of horror,
romanticize her, distort her to my image
than know the truth?

Nancy Peterson

How can I weed the garden with you,
talk about the weather,
before the other conversation takes place,
saying

>            hurt grievously
>            remember
>            sorrow deep
>            as the roots of the apple tree in Grandpa's back yard
>            beauty dark
>            as a rose forgotten after her bloom
>            remember

Have you had this conversation?
Can we have it now?

Mugs, I conjure you
sensitive, quiet, poet at heart.
What was your dream? Could sisters stand
up to brothers? Were you afraid
of your husband's touch? Where
did you go? Did you find demons
or friends? Did you have hope of getting
better? Did you leave your children
to protect them? Did the hospital or you
take your life?
I make much of our parallels.
You died at 42.
At 42, I begin to value the qualities in me
that were seen as defects,
the stream of consciousness that makes poetry.
Women who are vulnerable
are strong. Fifty years after you,
I can make the jump you couldn't.

Nancy Peterson

I know if you were here with me now, Mugs,
there would be comfort for you.
There would be women to
protect you, a host of angels
to surround you,
to lift you.

I am drawn
by the bitter silence
they give me about you.
You are the one
I want to know.

Is this out of fear,
that in my sorrow or old skin
they would leave me too?
Or out of a hope that in getting to
know you,
someone will,
in turn,
search for me?

I take in the potent silence.
I breathe out
to pink your flesh.

Nancy Peterson

# The Club

He beat me with the hem of a kimono
worn by a Japanese woman
this prized
painted
wooden statue
carved to perfection
in Japan or maybe Hong Kong.

She was usually on display
in our living room atop his bookshelf
among his other overseas treasures
I was never to touch.
She posed there most of the day
her head tilted
her chin resting lightly
on the white pointed fingertips
of her right hand
her black hair
piled high on her head
her long slim neck bared
to her shoulders.
An invisible hand
under the full sleeve
clasped her kimono close to her body
its hem flared
gracefully around her feet.

Mitsuye Yamada

That hem
made fluted red marks
on these freckled arms
my shoulders
my back.
That head
inside his fist
made camel
bumps
on his knuckles
I prayed for her
that her pencil thin neck
would not snap
or his rage would be unendurable.
She held fast for me
didn't even chip or crack.

One day, we were talking
as we often did the morning after.
Well, my sloe-eyed beauty, I said
have you served him enough?
I dared to pick her up with one hand
I held her gently by the flowing robe
around her slender legs.
She felt lighter than I had imagined.
I stroked her cold thighs
with the tips of my fingers
and felt a slight tremor.

Mitsuye Yamada

I carried her into the kitchen and wrapped her
in two sheets of paper towels.
We're leaving
I whispered
you and I
together.

I placed her
between my clothes in my packed suitcase.
That is how we left him
forever.

Mitsuye Yamada

# Genealogy

I come from alcohol.
I was set down in it like a spark in gas.
I lay down dumb with it, I let it erase what it liked.
I played house with it, let it dress me, undress me.
I exulted, I excused.
I married it. And where it went, I went.
I gave birth to it.
I nursed, I plotted murder with it.
I laid its table, paid its promises.
I lived with it wherever it liked to live:
in the kitchen, under the bed, at the coin laundry,
out by the swings, in the back seat of the car,
at the trashed Thanksgiving table.
I sat with it in the blear of tv.
I sat where it glittered, carmine,
where it burned in a blunt glass,
where it stood in a glittering lineup on the bar.
I saw it in the dull mirror, making up my face,
in the weekend silence,
in the smashed dish, in the slammed car door,
in the dead husband, the love.
Alcohol in the torn journal.
Alcohol in the void mirror.
My generations are of alcohol
and all I could ever hope to bear.

Joan Larkin

# Bottled

When Mother's drinking, the door to my room
slams shut, sealed with bottle labels.
Brown walls of glass, cracked mirror of moans,
blue curtains drawn, sewn closed with sobs.
No way out. Or in.

*How 'bout a drink?*

At five, sharp, let the masquerade begin.
What cunning disguises: Wear egg nog for
pleasing Santa, martini for praising the Lord.
Come, raise your voices. Dry! Dry!
Happy beerday to you. . . .

*Can I freshen that up?*

Our party's out cold, poor thing, its face
as pale as vodka. Every glass
is broken, every lamp lit.
Grenadine, you sad son-of-a-bitch!
Cocktail onion! Lemon twist! Stuffed olive!

*Can I pour you another?*

Sit down, won't you? Over there,
on that drunk—he's the sofa. Or that one—
he's a chair. Just give him a drink
before you sit. Then he'll be soft,
won't cause you any trouble.

Jill Breckenridge

*Just one more?*

When he throws his fist, the light
goes out. My room fills up with a jigger-
and-a-half, the furniture floats and bobbles.
Swallowed by this dark swirl, I swim
toward the blinking neon sign.

*Have a little nightcap?*

All the drunks are drowned. I can't find
a place to sleep. Ice cubes listen
to my psalms, chilled and swallowed
straight. Tuck me in, tuck me in.
I love you. You!

Jill Breckenridge

# Unlocking the Doors

1

One night, I saw a woman
jerk away from a man, run
for her life, but he ran faster.

"Get help!" I called to my friend,
ran after the woman. When she tripped,
he was on her, a big man, kicking
her ribs, her face,

then standing her up, walking her.
I caught up to them, took her arm,
asked, "Do you need help?"

"Willie," she pleaded, I looked at him,
repeated his name, "Willie,
she doesn't want to go,"

his fist clenched her collar.
I would not let go of her arm.

My friend brought two policemen,
I pulled the woman away. Crying
now, her head ached, her name
was Debbie from San Diego,
since fourteen she'd been on her own.

I kept my arm around her in the car.
They had one bed left at the shelter,
they took her in.

Jill Breckenridge

2

A man who beats his woman
arms himself with small excuses.

They have one plate, one fork,
one daughter between them,
share until the woman, careless,

drops the fork. She croons his name,
brushes his hair, sits quietly
next to him, but she can never

sit still enough; when he accuses,
she denies, his eyes dilate,
go steel, he raises his fist.

Who will hear her scream? She's alone
with a killer who will kill her slowly—

Later, he touches where the woman hurts,
marvels at her small wrists, the way
her hips hide jungles inside them.
He is always worse than he meant.

3

My own mother, her two black eyes,
her swollen upper lip,

how I wanted her arm around me
when we slept all night in the car,
coming in at dawn before the neighbors saw,
when we huddled in the bedroom,

Jill Breckenridge

him beating against the door,
the door bending toward us, groaning.

Night after dark night, I must
save her, even when she hits
first. How the small ones despise
weakness, he was what I loved,

what we both loved,
so when we hid in the bathroom
and she pressed her back against
his weight on the other side,

screaming, "No! No!"
to his, "Let me in!"

and when she made a bed
for me in the bathtub
out of soft pink towels,

even then I could not thank her,
she could not look me in the eye.

If now, in the light of morning,
she could finally unlock the door,
if only I could take her
by the arm and not let go.

———
Jill Breckenridge

# Lisa's Ritual, Age 10

Afterwards when he is finished with her
lots of mouthwash helps
to get rid of her father's cigarette taste.
She runs a hot bath
      to soak away the pain
            like red dye leaking from her
                  school dress in the washtub.
She doesn't cry.
When the bathwater cools she adds more hot.
She brushes her teeth for a long time.

Then she finds the corner of her room,
curls against it. There the wall is
hard and smooth
as teacher's new chalk, white
as a clean bedsheet. Smells
fresh. Isn't sweaty, hairy, doesn't stick
to skin. Doesn't hurt much
when she presses her small backbone
into it. The wall is steady
while she falls     away:
      first the hands     lost
arms dissolving     feet gone
    the legs    dis-      jointed
        body cracking down
           the center like a fault
              she falls inside
                    slides down like

*Grace Caroline Bridges*

dust     like kitchen dirt
                          slips off
      the dustpan into
                                      noplace

    a place where
nothing happens,
nothing ever happened.

When she feels the cool
wall against her cheek
she doesn't want to
come back. Doesn't want to
think about it.
The wall is quiet, waiting.
It is tall like a promise
only better.

_Grace Caroline Bridges_

# FIVE

"Then there is earth I say. . ."

—Christine Dumaine
"Second Language"

# Those Who Want Out

In their homes, much glass and steel. Their cars
are fast—walking's for children, except in rooms.
When they take longer trips, they think with contempt
of the jet's archaic slowness. Monastic
in dedication to work, they apply honed skills,
impatient of less than perfection. They sleep by day
when the bustle of lives might disturb their research,
and labor beneath fluorescent light in controlled environments
fitting their needs, as the dialects
in which they converse, with each other or with
the machines (which are not called machines),
are controlled and fitting. The air they breathe
is conditioned. Coffee and coke keep them alert.
But no one can say they don't dream,
that they have no vision. Their vision
consumes them, they think all the time
of the city in space, they long for the permanent colony,
not just a lab up there, the whole works,
malls, racquet courts, hot tubs, state-of-the-art
ski machines, entertainment . . . Imagine it, they think,
way out there, outside of 'nature,' unhampered,
a place contrived by man, supreme
triumph of reason. They know it will happen.
They do not love the earth.

Denise Levertov

# Picture from My Cousin

I wanted to write about these children on the beach, but what can I write except that Baiba is seven and Kristine is nine and Ruta is two and Peteris is six and Agnese is five, and they're my only two first cousins' children, and they live in a little town in Latvia, the same one where I was born, and they're all in a picture together as they picnic on the beach, and they're fairhaired, and some of them look alike and others don't, and the little one has a big white floppy ribbon on the top of her head, and she pouts and won't look at the photographer, and Baiba the seven-year-old has her finger in her mouth and her shadowed face looks pensive, and Peteris smiles at the camera, and Agnese scrunches her face up as she peers at the shiny lens and reaches for one of the strawberries in the big white enamel bowl, and she's wearing a little tee-shirt and little round baubles at the ends of her thin little pigtails, and it's all so normal, the cups, the thermos, the spoons, the big bowl of berries, the children after their swim, the summer grass tall behind them, the shrubs thick and dappled with light in the background, and I am filled with a pain and anger beyond words, because it's the summer after Chernobyl, and what secret death will they eat with each sweet berry, what danger hides in each drop of salt water they spit out as they come up from the glittering waves shouting, "Look, Ma, I can swim!"? And I want to shout, "Don't eat!" and "Don't swim in that water!" and it's too late, and what is the use, and my heart clenches with fear and with love for these children, the summer after Chernobyl.

Ilze Mueller

# Dust and Blue

All eyes watch the sky. The boring blue sky. No thunder-heads
rumble. No lightning rips the thin drabness of summer night. No
drama. No rainbow promise. The drought of '88 is kicking up the
dust. Top-soil from Saskatchewan fills the June sky, then drifts
along Dakota highways. Nature takes a hundred years to make an
inch of top-soil that rich and now it's blowing out through holes
in the Ozone. Some of the Old Ones say it's as bad as the Dust
Bowl time. Worse, some say.

In the parking lot of Rainbow Foods, the 100 degree heat radiates
from brownie-soft asphalt. Mirage people shimmer and quiver as
they move slowly to and from the cars. She walks toward me as if
I am the oasis. Her hair is sun-bleached, dried-up grass. Dust and
ash dull. Her calico dress has no color of its own, it looks tinted
like old photographs. Her chalky eyes are drained of pride. A ghost
with a never-ending duty. She holds the hand of a child, pulling
her toward me.

I know her, she's seeded my dreams with fear since I faithfully
said, "Now I lay me down to sleep . . ." every night, on my knees,
"God bless mommy and daddy and the starving children in India."
I grew up, cleaning my plate because once there wasn't enough.
It's a sin to waste. But now I'm not prepared. No money under the
mattress. No man to work for the W.P.A.

Cynthia Olson

She holds one hand out to me, the other hand holds tight to the child. Now I see that the child is real, full color. Sunny hair, pink warm cheeks, freckles across her nose, and her eyes sky blue. The ghost is bound to life. "Can you spare a few dollars, please, so I can get us a Greyhound ticket home, me and my kid." The voice is exhausted, expressionless, leaking through vocal cords. I can't answer, my scream doesn't work in nightmares . . . But she is walking away, even before she's done asking. Her hands full of dust and duty. The child, so real, obediently in tow.

Cynthia Olson

# For a Woman Murdered While Running at Land's End, October 1979

Late in the fall.
The clock rings and the man is already backing the car out.
I put up the shade.
Bare sky is streaked with red sandbars.
At dawn something slips
out of the room and the day begins.

We go our ways.
The truck comes to pick up the garbage, runs
a wheezy motor while I dress.
There's a light in a house through the trees.
This is the edge.
I could go that direction and be at the sea now.
I did it everyday in August.

Darjeeling in the cup. I leave the house.
The dome of the Russian cathedral is on top of the market,
an apple in a shooting gallery. Tattooed, a drunk
grabbed me on the midway once,
the boy beside me too slender to stop him
from smearing his mouth on mine.

I can't stop thinking of her.
The story gave her address. It made her seem close.
I carry some fruit in my lunch,
the death
in a newspaper folded on the seat of the car.

Patricia Kirkpatrick

She was running the cliff where the sea washes,
her legs thrusting the city behind her,
her voice out of anyone's reach.

I walk there when I want to
overlook the ocean,
its glistening points of pearl and smoky topaz.

I drive against the traffic.
I get over the bridge.
The day will be blue and smell like eucalyptus.
Sometimes a doe or buck
is heaped along the road.
She ran almost every day,
full-face into the sea wind, her breath
rising, falling
with the single arabesque of every step.
The strong light glazes pyracantha and wild radish
on this hill I'm passing.
It is hard to keep going.

*Patricia Kirkpatrick*

# Another Time Track

He's from another time track.
I leave mine behind when I go into his.
In there, they call me Mrs. M, mother of two daughters,
Ex-wife of Dr. M.
He never changes, he is Dr. G.
Has always been there; always there on time:
Seven-thirty sharp,
His pink face gleaming naked,
His hair a regulation crewcut
Just the way it was in boot camp and in dental school.
He comes in where I sit, clenched hands on arm rests,
Waiting for the worst,
Tackles a harmless topic, laid out with the rest
Of all his instruments—
How nights are getting nippy,
Soon winter will be here—
His hands choose shining probes.

How safe, how reassuring
The world becomes because
"We'll soon have that put right."

Every now and then a glimpse of Dr. G's
Private life. What he'd call private—
His wife had surgery
Last year, a hysterectomy.
"We got a second
Opinion. It was
The best thing for her. She's just fine now, yes."


Ilze Mueller

His daughter lives in Boston. Doesn't like it.
Would love to come back here. But her husband
Has a fine job there, and they signed
A lease they can't get out of.
His wife is off to Boston soon. Not Dr. G though.
She loves to shop. He hates it.
It's hunting season, too. He wouldn't miss it
For anything.

That's why each wall here
Has its own picture
Of ducks in flight.
That's where he gets away
From teeth, from shopping centers,
From the ruthless order of instruments
Laid gleaming side by side.
There's a short time each year
When Doctor G just sits
Under the sky, letting the wind blow on his face
And hears the cattails rustle
And listens to the geese
Calling to each other in those voices
That speak of wildness and of how
They all belong together.
Does he feel it too, a tearing in his chest
As though the call went out to him as well,
Does he raise his gun and sight
The bird among her fellows flying there,
Or do his hands sink?
Is the slow rush and thrill of this wild passing
Enough for him?

Ilze Mueller

# Chimayo

A dog ambles across the empty, dusty road
lifting his hind leg to pee on the garbage cans
of El Chimayo Café, where

BURRITOS  ✳  TACOS

HAMBURGERS

Y

GAS

are sold. Round, brown faces framed by crudely
lettered signs—a pink OPEN above, COCA COLA
in chartreuse below—peer out at us
from the concession stand as we drive up.
On the adobe, a painted hotdog trickles
crusty catsup and relish. We stop. Wait for gas.
Suddenly a car pulls up behind,
imprisoning us in the past. A woman cautions,
　　　¡Mira—tengan cuidado!

Pointing to our captor, she motions
little circles around her temple and mouths:
　　　Loco, loco,
　　　esperen hasta que se vaya.

Dogs in slow motion—salivating, panting,
like weary wolves—stop traffic as they sprawl
themselves across the road and lick their genitals.

Down here,
a brilliant heat subdues the evening,
while in the mountains, always the rain
falling in smudged streaks
·　like mammoth shades to earth,

Gloria Vando

204

and always God hiding
behind every dwarfed juniper bush, chamiza,
ready to spring on our smug Anglo skepticism
with some special sleight of hand—now
a simple dandelion, now a raspberry finch, all
ingeniously framed by a motionless sky,
the blue of my youngest child's eyes.

And far in the background a Rothko mural
of muted mountains surrounds us
with peaks of brooding greens, grays, lavenders
lapping and overlapping.   And always there
the hills; and always here the center, my center,
extending outward past the past,
far beyond the future—
for I was here before, even before
I drank the magic Chimayo potion
that obliterates time and space and boundaries,
restoring peace, oneness.

> I am the bear that comes at nightfall
> to greet the new moon
> soy india, soy mejicana
> soy mujer
> Soy yo.

Gloria Vando

# My First Memory, Switzerland, Circa 1947

I think I was not yet two
At home
In the tiny (neutral) country called
Switzerland
To which my parents escaped
& where I was born
& from which we later
Were forced to leave.
But then it was spring
& me so tiny, dark & so naked
Sitting bare bottom in a washtub
Of thin blue water
Under the impossibly high
Unreachable sky
Where my mother had left me
For just one minute alone
When the huge brindled cow
With her great
Arched nostrils came by
Snorting hugely
& drank up all my water.

Joan Dobbie

# Imagination

Here I am six years old in Sub B, sitting on the big rock.
Waiting for birds to fly.

Touching my chin and saying, "hm-hm." I'm wondering what it
would be like if you had wings to fly.

Hearing the mumbling of the cows in the green land.
Looking for blue windy sky, and the moving of the world.

Imagining seeing a beautiful woman with wings like an angel
formed by the clouds. She's wearing a white and gray gown.

Seeing a bright future, and my success ringing in my ears.
Shiny memory to take with me to travel around the world.

Dina Uahupirapi

# Fish Story: How Language Carries Us into the Unknown

*A priceless collection of music manuscripts, missing since WWII, has been located in Poland, traced by a British zoologist who spent five years searching for a herring's proper name.*

We practice our scales,
and when we wobble in the placing of a tone
we are ashamed, like civilized people
when they lose their balance
and wind up all over the place, taking up too much room.
We fade out, a human apology.
Meanwhile the fish rise and fall
in shameless glissando.
Fins shiver and linger in the curve
before the smooth downturn.

We lord it above them,
preen our throat feathers
and let the notes out.
When they catch a tuneful current,
we think we know how it goes,
neat black  ♪ 's riding an imaginary grid,
maneuvering for a good way.

"*Auf dem Wasser zu singen,*"
that's our cultural revenge
for not knowing our place
among fish and fowl.
We take Schubert out in a glass-bottomed boat.
The fish are quiet in their aquarium ponds.
They have secret names
but only we can sing them.

Brigitte Frase

# Inner Mongolia—The Grasslands

The road climbs steeply till it crests above the hills,
then the grasslands start, stretching across the earth's roof,
a green sea of swells and shadows.
The sky's so long, I read two weathers at the same time.

Wild yellow blooms, and buds that open into snow sprays
with red hearts. Clouds bunch above a pond,
sheep gathered below, the old shepherd
with his canvas raincoat open over tall cloth boots.
When I walk, the field explodes—a churr of wings,
grasshoppers. Frogs mutter on the pond's edge,
birds, the air itself hums.

Imagine a round padded yurt, sleeping in a flowered quilt
spread on the floor. You could move easily then,
roll up your home, and ride to catch this solstice moon,
to listen to the music of some other pond.

Pale circles ring the grass below the moon
as if horses ran there nightly, tracing its bright shadow.
Dusk now, one horse standing on the ridge,
dark against the last light. Two planets,
Mars and Venus, drifting past.

Imagine country thick and green and open as good love.
Imagine losing it in battle. Or worse,
giving it up like Wang Zhao Jin to stop the wars.
She married the Chinese emperor, rode south
past the broad-boned faces of her people
into the silk land of the Hans.

Sibyl James

209

I've seen those Chinese courts, walled cities
ornate with ceremony, every inch enameled.
Someone strums a *pipa* in the garden, someone
serves green tea, someone inks this on a scroll
rolled up and placed in carved chests.
Everything is beautiful, and still.

To honor Wang, her people built four tombs,
so long ago, they can't recall which holds her bones.
I know each tomb is empty. If I could rise
like moons and planets, I could see the rings
she traced each night around her country,
that circle of protection, keeping always on the edge
of longing, unable to swing home.

Sibyl James

# Santos and Stones

*Alma, te quiero que tú no eres ni gringa*
*ni hispana* and 2 spoonfuls of German,
from that *Nuevo México donde tu padre*
*con tus mismos ojos, tu* skin *y tu sangre*
would swallow a pinch of salt and make the sign
of the cross. Your mother: *coyote.*

*Vásquez, C de Baca, López, López*
your name a litany whispered into candles
on the way to *Chimayó.*
                              And the pilgrims still pray
to leave their crutches in the *santuario,*
even as the last *penitente* slides bloodsoaked
from sight. *Ancianos* still roam the highlands
and inhabit the houses and invite themselves
like meddling in-laws.

*Alma, mucho gusto que te veo* as you hurry
north beyond *Manzanos y Sandías,*
all the way home now, strong and forgotten
con Sangre de Cristo back in your spine.

*¿Eres tú* in the midday glare of mock-*adobe*
at the University? Is it you at the *Quien Sabe*
*Café,* red *chile* smell on the stove? *Dime,*
do I make you *más misteriosa* fingering the beads,
trudging in the heavy dark like *La Llorona?*
*Y todavía puedo querer que tú no eres ni gringa*
*ni hispana.*

J. Delayne Barber

¿Cuando te fábrico con palabras, estoy simplemente
usándote, como los dichos that have been used
before, como la gringa que viene to write her dissertation?
Sá, verdad. The truth breaks cool
como una estrella azul, whose luminosity
can be measured independent of distance.

I've entered the planetary sky
de tus ojos, charting your retrograde motion.
I follow you like a moon entre los sueños,
your past, los lugares que no puedes explicar.
In molten-light from the core, I finally see
que tú veas: país de arroyos y acequias,
of piñón-rivers and rockledges, desert edging las montañas,
cañón, volcano, mesa. It's your country.
Estoy aprendiendo la historia natural.
Even in sleep old words turn through your bloodstream
and you wake años oscuros de aquí.

¿Qué son tus recuerdos?
I have a snapshot of you crossing the footbridge
of the Acequia Madre, back to the mountain
you call Sleeping Giant, adonde la luz es útil
and illumines la lucha pa' una mujer
y su tierra amarilla, land full of weeds
and strange memories, donde el ráo le dijo "nada"
a la persona que estaba ahogando.
It is always the inarticulate struggle
como la tristeza que sientas pa' Zozobra
in the burning, when you have seen him laugh
and moan and yield nothing but the 4 seasons.

—

J. Delayne Barber

You might have ended elsewhere        •
than on that bridge, *Alma*, cupping the blue
of the sky in your father's hands.
*Esta fotografía I keep como una ficcion que yo creo*
*porque tú no eres ni gringa ni hispana.*

FOOTNOTES:

Hispanics use the term *"coyote"* frequently in New Mexico to
indicate someone of mixed heritage, along with its Native
American connotations. *Santuario de Chimayó* is a place one might
pilgrimage to for healing purposes. *Brotherhood of the Penitentes* is a
secret male religious order, members of which practiced
self-flagellation. *La Llorona* is a legendary wailing woman who
wanders the countryside at night, crying for her lost children.
*Zozobra*, or "Old Man Gloom," is a 60-foot-tall symbol that is set
afire and burned every September, complete with tape-recorded
moans and groans for added credibility. Zozobra weekend is
celebrated in Santa Fe as a fiesta for good harvest and good spirits.

J. Delayne Barber

# Foreigners

to Èva Ráth Stricker

When I meet Gustavo and Hilda,
their deep brown faces attract me like madrone
that saves in summer with its cool
glossy body. We are finding the land
as we talk: fig trees, dry california rock,
almonds and star thistle. Lorca's orange blossoms.
A certain light. His "fountain & laurel."
Dust that your feet know. All the small silver-green plants known:
yerba buena & sage. We sit down in the heat,
not strangers to this place, the country we carry
with our insufficient & suffering language, we give each other a
    home
believing against all evidence, no one will take this away.

Meredith Stricker

# Monarchs

All morning, as I sit thinking of you,
the Monarchs are passing. Seven stories up,
to the left of the river, they are making their way
south, their wings the dark red of
your hands like butchers' hands, the raised
veins of their wings like your scars.
I could scarcely feel your massive rough
palms on me, your touch was so light,
the delicate chapped scrape of an insect's leg
across my breast. No one had ever
touched me before. I didn't know enough to
open my legs, but felt your thighs,
feathered with red-gold hairs,
        opening
between my legs like a
pair of wings.
The hinged print of my blood on your thighs—
a winged creature pinned there—
and then you left, as you were to leave
over and over, the butterflies moving
in masses past my window, floating
south to their transformation, crossing over
borders in the night, the diffuse blood-red
cloud of them, my body under yours,
the beauty and silence of the great migrations.

*Sharon Olds*

# Second Language

If I must die young
let it be here on highway 34
stunned and quick, gone as a stray dog.
Let me think the last white lights
are egrets dipping in rain pools.
Let me come to death sticky and tired
from teaching Laotian refugees this language,
last words spent explaining *earth*
from the *earth*, becoming the moon,
turning in circles round a small
bent woman who, years in Thai camps,
cupped hands to catch the falling
heads of babies, taking
the slippery shoulders.

Then there is *earth* I say
lifting hands of Louisiana black.

Christine Dumaine

# Things Grow Up Out of the Dark

On the wall by the bathtub there clings
one barely discernible newborn slug, waving its tiny feelers
at the world. We call it the "slug hatchery,"
our ever-damp bathroom. The slug parents
six inches long and spotted like tropical
lizards come gliding up out of the silverware drawer
in the kitchen. I no longer scream when I see them. I even
consider them graceful. (Anything living is beautiful.) Outside
mushrooms abound and the roof is sprouting its yearly
green cover. We can expect at least six more months of this
fecund rain, and low sky, and the clacking
of my typewriter. Ducks mingle with sea gulls
in the schoolyard while I, like so many other
voluntary exiles from the frigid East
dream of snow this dark winter season.
                                        Oh not
just damp old sticky snow, the kind the grey sky
sometimes dumps, but real snow. Light snow. The delicate
North Country kind that demands temperatures
far below freezing and leaves you
breathless and sunblind like a child's over-bright memory
of Santa Claus. Cheeks cherry cold until
finally sometime around March it melts down
into "sugar snow" and trees that bleed
candy.
        With such blatant sentimentality I remember
all this glister. As though I'd actually
been a happy child. As though the tunnels
that we dug deep into snowbanks actually had led
to castles in those days. And princes. As though

Joan Dobbie

I didn't fly West with all my heart
packed into one small suitcase (uprooting my own children
in the midst of their childhood) and did it
because something that just might turn out to be beautiful
demanded to be born.

# In Western Massachusetts, Sixteen Months Sober

*The first year I was out here, because there were no flowers*
*I began picking up bones.*

—Georgia O'Keeffe

To find words for this.

There's a tree. And its shadow.
And a wind washing the shadow
uphill through the weeds.

Once you said to me,
*There's a word for everything.*
Words
I don't trust now.

I'm walking uphill—
no fiction.

Phrasebook of a country I'm visiting.
I remember the names from before.
Goldenrod, cricket. The cedar waxwing.
Driving downhill, a couple. Backseat, the kids.
The field blows toward me hard.

The late light chooses
white stones in the wall,
a white moth, and the white leaf
turning.

To simplify—
I tore so many papers.

Joan Larkin

Briefly
it was winter. Then
in Brooklyn, at the bottom of my house,
someone in the mirror
wearing my plaid robe,
still asking to be carried.

Walking home, the low sun
on my bare arms.
Outside the blind piano tuner's house
air stirs the flag,
a pony trots,
a boy watches his sister.

Francis, a year ago you asked,
*Do you have the willingness to be happy?*
I can't always say.
Today
I'm climbing this hill,
I'm picking up
this pen.

Joan Larkin

# SIX

"On this land, still marked with familiar
footprints . . ."

—Mary Crescenzo Simons
"Return to Mankiller Flats, Oklahoma"

# On Returning

Today I learn "tamarisk"
and cannot resist adding a flourish
of "feathery russet threads."
The dictionary deflates me
with "slender leaves, pinkish,"
so I let go of "burned rose,"
that romance of a color fading from itself.

From this strange window, longing
stutters homesick phrases.
It is bad at learning. It continues
to pronounce life
in the rhythms of loss, flight,
deviation from the ground note.

Before me, the plain leans down
as if to pick up something from the earth.
When it stands again, it is mountains
so far away they might be clouds,
until I call them
"*Berge.*"
Sharp ridges appear in the consonants,
vowels open their gentian mouths,
calling a lost child
learning its letters.

Brigitte Frase

The tamarisks wave lightly
beneath this window. In them,
need and have are soundless.
Tomorrow they will also be here,
absorbed in leaves, branches and roots.
When I disappear
in morning fog,
the mountains will go with me.

# Traveling Back

Traveling for the last time,
the old lady, purse around her neck
carry-ons dragging her arms,
de-planes vaguely, lost,
her eyes still viewing the Swedish coast
and Hälsingborg,
a strain of Buxtehude still organing her ear,
playing her back, back to see them all,
back to say goodbye
to her childhood's home and fields,
    *Hem och fält,*
so homely, so comely.

And never again: the stupid, 20-hour journey,
delays at Frankfurt, at London.
And never again: the arrival,
the flowers, the tears,
the babble of familiar accent
lulling her like a baby,
talking all night
with her childhood's best friend,
    *Midsommarafton,* Midsummer's,
in Dalarna. The dancing.

And ever again: the old songs,
strongly back.
    "Leaves are dropping
    In russet and gold.
    Green on the Baltic
    The waves ripple cold.
    Birches are bare . . ."

Sara Hunter

But was that really Swedish
or a granddaughter's song?
Baltic: *Ostersjön.*

*Kom, Flicka lilla, dansa* . . .
Come, little girl.
*Kom, lilla Mormor,*
Mother's Mother.

Bare all around her again,
claiming her back,
the Minnesota prairie
and burying ground.

Sara Hunter

# Obon: Festival of the Dead

On the day of the festival Uncle leads our
procession snapping his kimono sleeves as he swings
his arms. My cousins and I carry fresh-smelling
wooden buckets filled with garden flowers over our
arms like picnic baskets. Aunty motions to me with
the broom and rake in both hands, hurrying me along
as I lag behind on new wooden *getas*.

At the gravesite together we scrub the family
headstone, weed, sweep and rake the ground around
under Aunty's firm command and Cousin Fumiko
whispers in my ear she is not my real mother, my
real *Okaasan* is here, we are taking her home today.

I watch the only Aunty I know who is arranging
masses of flowers about the grave in slow motion
until Uncle in quaint country dialect barks, "*Sorede
yoka.*" That's enough. He kneels at the grave
and in formal language reserved only, I
suppose, for deceased wives says, "*Omukae ni
kimashita, sa-a sa-a ikimasho.*" We have come to
take you home. Come, come, let us go.

I am told to cup my hands behind my back to carry
*Obasan* home. At nine I feel too old for childish
games but I play anyway. I am the only child here.
In America her name will be read on Sunday during
Prayers for the Dead but over here I am trying to
balance the spirit of *Obasan* on my back
clattering over pebbled roads back to the village.

Mitsuye Yamada

We entertain *Obasan* royally all day on this
sweltering August day. Aunty has prepared her
rival's favorite dishes: *udon*, steaming hot noodles
in clear soup; *imo*, sweet potatoes baked on hot
charcoals; and *omanju*, sweet dumplings. Her place
is set with chopsticks on the left side. Uncle says
she was a *"wagamama no onna,"* a self-centered
woman, but my Cousin Fumiko shakes her head, her
eyes glistening and says, "She was only
left-handed." I make a note of this in my mind to
tell my left-handed brother back home in America
"Believe it or not way over there in Japan we had
one maverick aunty who used chopsticks with her left
hand too!"

After dinner we take *Obasan's* treasured silk
*kimonos* out of tissue papers. We girls are
transformed into singing, dancing maidens. Cousin
Fumiko teaches us *Obasan's* favorite songs and
dances. We make a place for her and play her
favorite games. When she loses, my cousin whines
just like her late mother, *"Kuyashii, kuyashii,"* I
hate it, I hate it. Aunty and I, strangers
together, have come to know the real *Obasan* on this
day, *Obon*, Festival of the Dead.

Mitsuye Yamada

227

At dusk we carry *Obasan* on a handcrafted boat to
the beach and join a hundred other villagers with
their own dead. The priests in tall hats and white
robes standing knee-deep in water chant their
blessings over our vessels. *Obasan's* boat lists
and sways in the water from the weight of too many
*omanju* we had loaded for her long journey back to
her place of rest. Uncle lights the torch on the
bow and pushes her out as he coaxes, "*Ike, ike,*" Go
on, go on. Her sharp bow cuts the water as she
joins the shoal of lights out to sea.

My cousins call out, "*Sayonara Okaasan matta rainen
ni neh?*" Goodbye Mother until next year? Aunty dabs
her eyes with her handkerchief says, "*Anta shiawase
da neh?*" Aren't you lucky? I nod in confusion. The
sky is aflame as thousands of silent Roman
candles float out with the tide.

Mitsuye Yamada

# Put a Woman into the Memory Box

Steady in the darkness
of the field outside the window.
I know them by their breath,
the cows, the hot scratchy soughing,
of the absent-minded jaws
grinding grass into food, blood,
life       that absent-minded grinding.

I feel like a tender sausage
between fat eiderdowns.
Ironed lace edging the pillow,
a porcelain jug
within languid reach.
Milk, grass, water,
goose down and pillowed sleep.
There is more safety here
than I can ever use.

Old smells insinuate. They know me
after thirty years,
two continents, an ocean.
The pump glimmers in the cool sheen
of the first moment
I stood before it. And the currants
behave as if these same tart berries
had already plunged through my lips,
my sharp young teeth.

Brigitte Frase

Why won't these things be quiet in their nature?
Dumbness is their calling. By what sleight
of mind do they summon me?
My presence here is half conjurer's trick.
Put a woman into a memory box,
out slides a girl.
In her future, no cows
graze by the light of street lamps,
nuzzle the board under the mattress. Why
do they call her then? Why
do they need me?

Cows! In the years of exile
from the language I first saw you in
I have gathered books and pleasures,
poems and sorrows.
I have been worn by the edges
of useless facts and two-faced ideas.
Nothing particular wishes me
either well or ill.
Bullies of the real push sharp prongs
into my skull, but do without meaning it
a lovely thing . . .
they startle awake all the little gray cells—
the sentinels of reason,
the fussy archivists,
the sleeping beauties of imaginary kingdoms—
and they find themselves,
as now,

gazing quietly at your image.

Brigitte Frase

# Searching for Schüpfen

It's not just Schüpfen she's looking for,
it's either something so large, like desire
for an absent love, or so small
like a hair, finding Schüpfen
will not do. Outside Berne, she thinks

is where to look, but since the trip
may be too simple, the search end
too quickly, she will start in Paris
take the train south and east
to the city near the village of her mother.

She has so little history to go on—
her mother an orphan raised
by neighbors, animals brought into the house,
skiing out second-story windows
for the few years of school. Each piece

of paper reveals a different name:
Marta Rose, Marie, Rosa and *no last name
but guesses from the cousins*. No fixed date
among the spread of years. *Meadow, stream*,
beyond the railroad station, fields

Dona Luongo Stein

stretch out to woods. It's the future
she wants to make whole for the grandchildren
to grow into. She will have made a circle,
pulled a fine thread from the past through
field, eidelweiss, goat bells as she checks

names on the mossed stones in the churchyard
then lists in brown ink on baptismal books.
She'll tell each child what the flowers smell like
and if there's a name, the name.

Dona Luongo Stein

# Returned American

I stare out of the long windowed house
into the blank look
of the lost hotel across the square

*ban a tighe*
they have taken to calling me
*woman of the house*

I avert its unblinking eyes,
like those of a mourner
in this country where death is a cult

and Cait
dismissing Kathleen
as far too formal

my eyes go where the fields go
to meet the steeple
that gives the road up there its name

and *Cathain*
in old Irish
the real name, at last

Five generations stare out of me
unburden themselves in my gaze
all wanting to know
as they drink in the sight

and they tell me
that "them that went out

Kathleen Cain

233

why they are so thirsty
for this day
and the simple line of river

                            don't hardly ever come back"

and the road
and the trees in the rain

Kathleen Cain

# Return to Mankiller Flats, Oklahoma

for Cherokee Chief Wilma Mankiller

Another Trail of Tears,
from our Adair, Oklahoma farm to San Francisco,
moving us again, to live in a hotel
and work a strange land.

Objects of the blue-veined are foreign to native hands,
telephones and elevators, skates and hula hoops and the T.V.
My sister and I read aloud, imitating sounds of those who fit,
becoming fluent in the San Franciscan tongue.

The memories of pie suppers, my mother's garden,
the ever present stranger in greater need
whom Dad would bring home,
now provide my direction on the return trail.

There have been other trails, of broken bones
and lifeless limbs, ones of crutches and determination,
others lining the heart, wrapped and suspended between trees.

Further trails of tears, bleached by erosion
from white-eyed stares, once inroads forged by Cherokee women
who ruled the tribe before our traditions
were blanched along the way.

On this land, still marked with familiar footprints, I return
to fight a war, not on the battlefield but in the empty pockets
and bellies of those whose spirits walked before.

Mary Crescenzo Simons

# Exile's Letter: After the Failed Revolution

A world exists beyond the limits of this pane,
out of sight, but not out of mind.
Truly, there are higher vistas, better gazebos,
miraculous avenues beyond these closed doors.
Not to mention, a poet humbler and kinder than myself
somewhere between Cold Mountain and Lake Lopnor—
who may never write again, and for whom
the sun rises and sets only peripherally now. . .
as she threshes wheat or forces silk from mulberries,
not hers—as she walks into exile vowing no return—
she looks up, finds my face in the moon, smiles,

> "Dear Cousin, do not mourn me or this empty sky,
> for the sky is limitless. Ah, yet, there is a limit
> to even 'sky'. Like them, we are fallow deers . . .
> on Regret Road we must not tarry."

Marilyn Chin

# The Other Side

to Èva Ráth Stricker

The country she inhabits, where pale people
wait in line on the other side, could you call them alive?
Their speech—quirky, hobnailed as hunting boots
& sooty train stations. A language with special words
for red tulip embroidery, sheepskin flasks, a carriage
covered with furs. And these scalloped edged photographs
of thoroughbred horses, a lake rimmed by poplar trees.
Relatives hold up their babies in the half shade
& almost convince us that the others—the missing ones—
are alive—in another place, like ours, but with different
food: poppyseed & thick sour cream, curved Balaton fish.
We could almost believe the letters cross over
as a spadeful of dirt carried across is believed.
Willow sticks in the mail. Proof we can speak to each other,
bridging—a parallel city—her city of bridges.
I am signaling to a place in your country. Your underworld
streets, how bright & real they seem to you
as you cross the stage, cross the mirrors
in a saffron dress, turning and returning.

Meredith Stricker

# SEVEN

"The more a thing is torn,
the more places it can connect."

—Meredith Stricker
"ISLAND"

# The Seed Is the Light of the Earth

for Muriel Rukeyser, October 1981

In the absence of light
we maintain our eyes cannot see.
We believe our pupils dilate
to a maximum degree and no more.
We are certain our bodies do not glow
with the cold phosphorescence of the bog,
of water, unfathomed, under pressure,
our own, or beyond our making. We assure
ourselves we are exonerated because
we cannot float through the night
graceful with inherent sonar. We think
anatomy keeps us from the dark forest.

I tell you here, in this dark, this
indistinct country, comes our shaped
and fleshed evolution. That step
on the unlit path stretches us,
and those who may come after.
With each hesitant journey
we open, blazing beacon fires,
flashing lanterns from high, distant
hills. Dark surrounds us. We are
paradox. We carry our own light
and move in love through the dark,
as the seed loves the earth enclosing it.

Christina Pacosz

# Macenattowawin (Birch Bark Biting)

*Raven Gallery, Minneapolis*

The white bark is peeled from the birch. The layers pulled apart. A piece is folded in half and then half again. nvuelzjch takes the point of it in her mouth. She bites along the fold. Eyeteeth against side-teeth. She chews a geometric design in the papery bark. A braille of sorts. Something like a large snowflake when she unfolds it. Maybe the pattern of woodland blizzards still in her head. The old woman has chewed so long her teeth are gone. The spirits come to her in bifocals. Together they enter the chaos before creation. They feel their way back through the dark. The birch-bark biter hears the ancestors in their graves. Sometimes they grind their teeth in sleep. She holds to the spirit ahead of her. Her dentures now chewing. Does it matter the earth has changed? nvuelzjch still has the journey, bringing her bitings from the dark.

*Diane Glancy*

# The Move 5 Houses Down the Street in a Day

Iron horse. Ah ho. Iron lung. Rattling the air. Squeezing out smoke. Yellowed as light through old window shades. In the room now the head cries. The heart tells it to hang on. How always in the past it had to leave what it was. How the heart has worked for generations. Angels without a pinhead to dance on. Ancestors walking to a new land. The little cornrows of teeth. The open field of the head. All night the heart hears the train moving. It waits for heaven to open and it does. How else would this load get to there? The rows of books. Dishes. The beds. Chairs. Sofas. No. The open heaven is like a wound. The pus of angels appears. Do they carry boxes? The thoughts ask. Can they lift tables? Will they put on the arms and legs that came off? The heart reminds the thoughts they are wiped by the lamb. The mop of angels. Their handkerchiefs always under the nose. The pins sticking worry. The nurse of the heart saying soon it will get well.

Diane Glancy

# Harlem

There was little more that summer
than gray pigeons in light-flecked
ginkgos, but there was
that, and we remarked on the light—
how the pigeons shook it loose
and trailed it down Lenox—
as if the sun had finally risen

over Harlem. And the hymns
those Sunday mornings like sighs
to Jesus or the naked
wishes of earth—naked
hands on backyard porches
clapping up storms, thunder
familiar as birthpain.

And the gospels inside
of sex and breakfast, soft
dishwater in the sink, how
we broke the glass of old
reflections and sprinkled ourselves
with the joy of salvation.
Little more that summer than

two women moving in love
near the fragile bones of old men
stacked in bombed-out doorways—
sweet God in heaven—
it was all we could do
to keep ourselves from burning up,
so hot the sun in our hearts.

Maureen Seaton

# She Drives

And drives like she is living
In a movie. A man on the radio sings
Being good is not good enough.

The tachometer glows. Phone poles
Necklace into the big sky; a hot dry wind
Flirts with her windows, with speed.

She remembers to keep her eye
On the distance. For a moment the dark
Empty space beside her fills

With retribution, for a moment the road
Seams up behind her. But then houses flash by,
Like scrawled notes pinned to the wall;

A shopping bag left on the front step,
A dog on the walk. Ornamental
Deer shimmer on the lawn,

Relentless, open-mouthed, grazing.
Bright kitchen windows, a hand
Offered across the table.

Sophie Cabot Black

# The Doomsayers

Some say because the tallest pine
beside her bedroom window is infested
this autumn with borers, and some say
because elm leaves have blown again
into the gutter and backed-up
her sewer

And some say because there is black
blood on her son's pillow every morning
and some because the orange-striped
kitten with the white chin was poisoned
by her neighbor

Some think because she owns a pink satin
coverlet in which she delights
and many perfumes—patchouly, cedarwood,
attar of roses, vanilla of benzoin—
in which she indulges,
and she suffers too little

Some claim because everyone listens
to her and some claim
because no one listens to her

And some because the man who believes
in her work and praises her work
kills chickens by raping them
after midnight in his back room

Pattiann Rogers

And some because all flowers—bog orchid,
glacier lily, twisted stalk, desert parsley,
even the iris—are just recent
evolutionary developments, and she knows it,
and some because the sun is dying, will
disappear—bloated shell, shriveled pit,
microscopic ash—in ten billion years,
and she knows it, knows it

And some say because she is not a man
and some say because she is not a woman

And some because her endeavor is too vain
and some because it is too implacable and some
because it is too heavy and some because
it weighs nothing

And they are wrong, all of them.
Wrong!

Pattiann Rogers

# Epiphany

My church is filled with snow
and women, blinded,
chant the old somber hymns
of sin
that must be washed in blood.

The water of life
in the baptismal font
has frozen
and snow drifts around the marble altar
where a figure mumbles,
lifting dry bread
to the heavens.

Take, eat,
the body and the blood,
the crucified whose death
brings everlasting life—
a mystery
that curses flesh.

I watch the eternal flame go out,
then turn away.
On the back wall of this Christian church,
through the paint,
through the plaster that has hidden
thousands of years,
a fresco shines.

Nancy Paddock

It is She
who has been humbled,
dismembered and despised,
who would lift my head
from ages of cold sleep

and rides upon my back
until I burn beneath the moon
and dance,
though all round
the earth is undermined
by graves.

I kneel,
baptized, in a rush
of melting.

Nancy Paddock

# How She Operates

I       She holds you by the hair,
        dunks your face
        into the cold sky of morning,
        pierces your eye with sun.
        She prods you in the back.
        Time to get moving on the journey.

        She tells you
        Arctic terns continue
        on their flight, iguanas
        reproduce themselves,
        wildflowers penetrate the rock,
        and so on. Did you think
        you were an exception?


II      She also uses a softer approach.
        Wary of sudden gentleness,
        you cup your hands across your heart
        to keep Her out, grit your teeth
        against the offered broth.
        But you forget your usual
        cynical remark.

*Grace Caroline Bridges*

She flaunts another sunset,
the wide fiery panorama;
you manage to give only a glance
from the corner of your eye.
Later you dream:
a single egg cracks open,
out swim countless scarlet fish
wriggling upstream together, you
quickest among them all
flashing and flashing your tiny scales.
You twitch in sleep,
wake hungry.

III       She allows appetite
to press its advantage
as you warm your hands
around the fragrant bowl.
You take the spoon, saying
this is not surrender.

She smiles, knowing
you will soon be ready
for creatures scurrying across the sand,
patterns of sand, sand
on the bright blossom,
on your skin,
your skin not yet waiting,
not yet the kiss.
All in good time.

*Grace Caroline Bridges*

# Dialogue on Finding Someplace To Live

*after Anne Sexton*

When we were small we could call anything home
hollow trees
crotches of live oak
nests of high fern by the creek
refrigerator box
closet underneath the stairs' backbone
quilted tent, with flashlight
                (aunt's cathedral quilt, yet, brother's flashlight
                  rent-free until they were needed—or *discovered*)
old rudderless boat holding canopy of willow, or,
at night, when they moved in, stars alone.

Those homes came ready-made, perfect, arrived
and went as turtle shells, each new
as the garden's morning web
or a fresh-painted yellow kitchen. Someone
we knew had a formal child-sized bungalow
with portico, puce shutters, curtains, and floor
she could sweep before tea parties
or after storms
when solitary or clumps of leaves littered
or grit began to migrate underfoot.
                        The woman that girl
is now peers out at the drawing moon remembering something
embedded in the dark side of the mirror, or forgotten
in a bowl of flowers; this cousin cannot sleep unless in boat
on the open sea, at least not deeply.
                      One playmate now
drives miles and pays to speak to a white room
about definitions of *hunger, promise, fury, August*

Lori Storie-Pahlitzsch

and she leaves each time with words for terrible, cripple, miracle;
her spirit and body do not get along.

We move by arbitrary signals, to new shell, box
winnowing, finding a place to live.
When we were little we could call anything home.

Lori Storie-Pahlitzsch

# Original Mind

*The kingdom of god is spread upon the earth*
*and people do not see it.*


Though the world fills with sorrow and rage,
though news of poison, destruction, disaster
erupts into the living room,
though death rattles
off the pages of the newspaper,
though talks to forestall the end of the world
break the peace—

Delight comes,
unbidden.
All
the human world of pain
dissolves.

The morning light is new each day
to sleep-washed, open eyes
and infant fascination.

This is real. We are born and reborn
to delight
in this world. The baby,
out of what great well of inborn humor, laughs
and that pure, rippling
original chuckle, straight from the belly,
is delight.

She laughs, so easily amused,
at me, at all of us.


Nancy Paddock

We are all hilarious
in our sadness. We are fools,
gone blind to glory,
stumbling over the very roots
of paradise.

Nancy Paddock

# Report from Another Country

A friend writes, "We're not talking about any port
in the storm." Most of us are specific,
in search of a script that when offered, can't be refused.

Our river life is complete. The fish are healthy.
We swim in it and young lovers meet on the banks at night.

Clearly, we don't want to be the victims of our own fantasies
nor desire the most feared,
to be overcome by the long lost echoes of our pasts
that return on us without gain, programmatic, unrefined.

Our hardest prejudice is the one we have against ourselves.
For me, I look to the end of hiding from myself and others.

Lately, from across the river, come the copiers,
with rulers, T-squares, magic assembly lines.
They offer a new world.

Tonight we will all meet at the mouth of the river
and tell stories we might forget later,
after the old men who come to reproduce us
play us songs
that will make our feet tap and tap until nothing else matters.

Charlene Langfur

# For the Record

in memory of Eleanor Bumpers


Call out the colored girls
and the ones who call themselves Black
and the ones who hate the word nigger
and the ones who are very pale

Who will count the big fleshy women
the grandmother weighing 22 stone
with the rusty braids
and a gap-toothed scowl
who wasn't afraid of Armageddon
the first shotgun blast tore her right arm off
the one with the butcher knife
the second blew out her heart
through the back of her chest
and I am going to keep writing it down
how they carried her body out of the house
dress torn   up around her waist
uncovered
past tenants and the neighborhood children
a mountain of Black Woman
and I am going to keep telling this
if it kills me
and it might in ways I am
learning

Audre Lorde

The next day Indira Gandhi
was shot down in her garden
and I wonder what these two 67-year-old
colored girls
are saying to each other now

planning their return
and they weren't even
sisters.

*Audre Lorde*

# Jerusalem Shadow

*for we were strangers in exile*

imagine the desert   the cast of light
imagine the day breaks at sundown
imagine the thirst and the cool water

in the desert   imagine you never left
the village never burned   your voice
was never too loud       imagine

you never lugged children and bundles to the sea
for a boat   to anywhere
never entered blond neighborhoods
never timed by the sun       imagine

you   in the desert   dark
as your darkest cousin   everyone's hair
is coarse and wild   the oil on your skin

is good   for something
in the desert   imagine you never left
your people have been here for centuries
places are named for them

—

Melanie Kaye/Kantrowitz

so the plane sweeps down into the desert
imagine breaking open to hold
what the desert holds

but you're a stranger
the language blurs like any unknown tongue
you feel stupid   straining your ear   for sense   you eat

cake   lots of cake *uga* and say
*tayeem meod*   very tasty   and it is   but then
you're silent   your vocabulary exhausted

and the people   familiar   not
strangers   but still
you have to meet them one by one

slow   imperfect
like any human encounter

———

I sit drinking tea on the balcony of the house you were raised in
where evenings your grandparents   cousins   sipped tea
told stories in Ladino   but you are named in Hebrew   *Chaya*
meaning *life*   the sun washes my skin
you talk of walks through East Jerusalem
of the lost backpack returned intact with a gift of fresh *pitot*
these things changed you   opened you   you fill my cup again
it's morning on the *Rechnov Nisim Bekhar* in West Jerusalem
Jewish Jerusalem
I am your guest   you are yourself
not a mirror   not a statistic

*Melanie Kaye/Kantrowitz*

this might be my home   but is not
I was born all over the planet   this time in Brooklyn
I came here looking for the seas to part   and truth
to rise up   wet
and obvious

I sit on the pink-grey stone by the Damascus Gate   eating hummous
the sun is lavish   direct   you sit one step up dressed in a black
   robe
a white headdress   beside you a boy   *my brother,* you tell me   later
after we catch each other's eyes   after we smile once
and again   until you pat the stone by you   motion for me
to come sit   your name is *Ma'ha*
you want the English word for my sunglasses
for the digital watch you wear with your black robe
you say, *you like hummous?*
I nod   smile   speak neither English *yes* nor Hebrew *ken*
though I'm sure you know *ken*   I don't know *yes* in Arabic
I think you know I'm a Jew
your watch shows 12:01
it's noon by the Damascus Gate in East Jerusalem
Arab Jerusalem   I am your guest   you are yourself
not a victim   not a symbol

—

Melanie Kaye/Kantrowitz

*Yerushalayim*

waking on *Nisim Bekhar* in the golden city

if I walk the winding streets
in the clear gold light

if the past is written on pink-grey stone
tablets   the walls of the city
houses   polished in blood

if the future is billowing
formless

shall I count the windows in Kiryat Arba
and call them facts

or discount the nights in shelters at the Northern edge—
are these not facts?

and the Litani
and the desert's need—

are these not facts?

—

Melanie Kaye/Kantrowitz

### Yerushalayim shel zahav

I came here looking for home or exile
not both

I came here looking for women
but there are men in front

the Arabs   without their *kaffiyehs* would pass for Jews
the Jews   without their *kipot* would pass for Arabs

the *Hasidim* who walk to prayer when the day
dips into *shabat*

the Muslims   washing their feet to enter
the Mosque   radiant over the city

and the Mosque was nearly blown up
like the Jewish bus   like the Arab bus

enter the market   they check my pack for bombs
this is a fact

—

I came here seeking a thread
and see a shadow   or is it a woman
or two women   shifting back and forth on the same spot

looking alike   though at first you
wouldn't see it   the hair   skin   language close
almost comprehensible   *shalom*   *salaam*

Melanie Kaye/Kantrowitz

and which is the stranger
whose flesh was torn
who grabs whose sleeve
who eats dark bread and potatoes
whose teeth stain dark from the tea
whose tongue was formed abruptly in kitchens
in whispers   quick   quick

and which century do I mean
when does one woman become the other
when does the rooted one who belongs transform
into the one forced out
when does the one forced out   and out   and out
return   to force out
and when does the other return
and how

———

here are some facts:

    peace is not an absence

    victims are not ennobled

    home is the storm's eye
    unless the stranger   too   is welcome

    we were strangers in exile

    a people is bound in memory

    I thirst   for my people

Melanie Kaye/Kantrowitz

—

*borukh ato adenoy elohenu*

let my people in
to history

let me not wait outside

let me not freeze in the posture of victim

let me break open to hold
the *khet-raysh* sound
the goat-honey smell
the light on the stones of Jerusalem
where I lived on hummous   and sweet dark tea

let my people heal

*omeyn*

5745-5746

Melanie Kaye/Kantrowitz

# This Spring

The dissent of trees over the space of roots.
The dissent of measurements and the names
of things,
the color of the intruder's eyes.
The dissent of days congealing
divisions, silences, the hoarded script
of leftover dreams. The dissent of us
determining everything. Everything,

you say. And nothing. We face each other
across the swollen distance of dissent.
Strangers. In a foreign land—these
rooms we call ours. Our
mouths broken. Your face dark
with the color of my voice,
and the days, disfigured, unsightly, go
on with their dying. At midnight
nothing left but a jack's throw of stars
in the cold spring nights. Beyond reach,
somewhere,

something turning slowly green, and holy.

Regina deCormier-Shekerjian

# The Edge

I set the shorelines of the world by perpetual decrees, so

are not our own edges **that**

contain our energy and keep **the**

outside forces at bay like shores of the **oceans**

whose boundaries are always in motion? Even **though**

the waters remain, **they**

can be as gentle ripples or as towering waves that **toss**

giant logs like toothpicks; **and**

when our inner seas **roar**

and our own tides ebb, we **can**

remember the seashore: **never**

settled. In the most deadened times that come to **pass**

we can pray for the return of energy and the will to live, **those**

gifts that come through grace, which has no **bounds**

Jeremiah 5:22

Sandra Price

# Then

And what of afterlife? I comfort
myself as I comfort myself with a
new dress. Aren't I wearing it now?
I will have a new body also. I'll
ask directions to the ancestors'
house. Sometimes I can almost see
the road, that dark place between the
street-light of the stars. Hey yota.
It will be striking. The renewal of
it all. The reunion with those I've
lived without. The hope I hold in my
hands. The revival of our stories.
I've heard ghosts of them rattling
the attic at night. And the Great
Spirit whom I've felt, yes, when I
look out the window and see a bird
scratching his head with his foot,
and thought if only I could do that.
The Great Spirit always walking on
the other side, the other dimension,
and there was no way through. But
someday, he kept saying, someday, as
we walked. I only had to wait for
that time when I saw the end and it
would be the passage to where I'm
going anyway. Now I have a token for
the gate. I can reach through the
invisible wall and know the after-
life. You see I should not have made
it this far. This world is a
fraction. My way of life folded and
put away like a leaf or wildflower in
the pages of a book. I won't know

*Diane Glancy*

it until later. That life I feel
moving somewhere just outside the
body. It's mine. I just can't touch
it yet. Nor see except sometimes the
image I bring back from a dream.
Then I feel the moccasins on my feet.
The feathers in my braids. I hear
my grandfather singing his holy song
for me. Yeh toh. There was not the
build-up of generations, the having
time to tell it to the next. There
was not the old trails paved but
looking again for the land and the
road to make through it. Not the
overlap of what we'd done, but kept
from coming together, the buffalo
robe up there in the drawer of the
clouds. The hallway, the front door,
the steps out to the sky where
everything looks smaller the farther
away it is. But it's only each
previous day growing small, the
harvest of it gone so always from
nothing again we feel our way, the
Great Spirit saying here, this way,
now more toward that.

Diane Glancy

# Coyote's Disguise as a Man Is Up

Coyote eats a tuna sandwich at her desk. She picks the crumbs of wheat-bread from her hairy chest. Hurriedly she puts them in her mouth. What a portfolio. The mouth between lips with the two rows of teeth inside. What a whizz the creator was. Only he knew how to build a mouth. The tongue carrying food into it, sending the word out. The Word. Just think. The little truth of life. What else could be done at this end? The beginning. More than the eye. Was the mouth. Ho to to. Hum ro hum. Her days of model airplanes were over. No more flying in her room always bordered by the ceiling. No, now she was in air. Exiled from the earth. Its dominion of gravity. She no longer had to be he. Now she was Life itself. Star of Texas. Blessing and grassitude.

*Diane Glancy*

# Kneading Bread

*for Denis on a day when there is no money*

There is a rhythm to it
folding the dough over
the fluid motion
of the heel of your hand
do not be afraid
fold it over and over
push it away
with the heel of your hand
When I was young
Grandma Marguerite made biscuits
and her mother before her
the dark loaves of the old world
Grandma Ruby in Mississippi made cornbread
served up with blackstrap and jam
do not be afraid
In India and Palestine
women make bread without kneading
and in Mexico and Guatemala
there is crushing and grinding of corn
do not be afraid
keep up the rhythm
and we will talk, my son,
of bread that will fill us
soon with the aroma of life
and grain the first fruits
of all people
do not be afraid
a rhythm to it
this kneading to stay alive
my son, you will know
what before only a daughter would learn

Teresa Anderson

how to survive inside this rhythm
centuries of women making bread
the rhythm of it
and the fluid motion
with the heel of your hand
do not be afraid
we are living
we sing and fight
and shed tears for our children
we the kneaders of bread
we the grinders of corn
we the sowers of wheat
in the shadow of missiles
we who survive
in the rhythm of it, my son,
do not be afraid

And in the name of
the woman who walks in shadows
the woman denied shelter
in the name of
the woman forced from her homeland
the woman who sifts ashes for revenge
in the name of
the woman who searches for food
the woman who sees children burning
in the name of
the woman who tends ravaged fields
the woman who gives birth in exile
in the name of
the woman who sings us to sleep

*Teresa Anderson*

in the name of
the woman who tends the fire
in the name of
the woman whose hands bring healing
the woman who refuses to bow down
in the name of
the woman who turns to the Mother of God
the woman whose child dies in her arms
in the name of
the wound and fire of her longing
I promise you
we will all return
There is a rhythm to it
folding the dough
over and over
the fluid motion
of the heel of your hand
do not be afraid.

The Feast of the Transfiguration
August 6, 1985

Minneapolis

Teresa Anderson

# ISLAND

to Èva Ráth Stricker

Taken away from her language
she is islanded in white
space, beautiful dove island,
the poor body stranded here
wants to speak her first
sounds: égy ketö haram,
the numbers, négy öt hat—
all broken away from her
so that she may live.
They tell her she is lucky,
when so many others have perished,
now her tongue translates
automatically. She is lucky
to live like Eurydice
not dead exactly—just displaced.
We try so hard to stay alive, above ground
but it's not clear if the earth
will survive us, we love her so much,
our gaze dissolves her—some of her water,
some of her air—we could even blow her up
all at once, the way Orpheus
loved Eurydice. I hated him
for looking back, but he is no safer
than any one of us, our Orpheus,
torn, & acrid vines burn, bleeding from empty
sockets, his head, his lyre wash up on Lesbos,
"thy floating singer late" & where
did Hart Crane wash ashore—
his head, his lyre floating forever in the word.
The more a thing is torn,
the more places it can connect.

Meredith Stricker

The poor body—fragile as Sappho's lost
text, taken from her language into
another life? We want to believe
it will never end
it will never end.
Already we are swimming toward
an island we say we can never drown
if life stays alive, we will read
her back to us, whole again, if life
survives us, the body will
be our book & keep on
singing.

Meredith Stricker

# Biographical Information

Marjorie Agosin is a Chilean writer living in exile in the United States. She is the author of several books of poems, including *Zones of Pain* and *Women of Smoke*. She has recently edited a collection of fiction by Latin American women writers, *Landscapes of a New Land*, for White Pine Press. Her translator, Cola Franzen, has translated the work of several Latin American writers including the work of Marjorie Agosin.

Teresa Anderson is the author of *Speaking in Sign*, West End Press, and translator of *A Call for the Destruction of Nixon*, by Pablo Neruda. She's worked in Poets-in-the-Schools in New York, Oklahoma, Minnesota, and Texas.

J. Delayne Barber was born in Georgia. She received her B.A. from the University of New Mexico, and her M.A. in Creative Writing from the University of California, Davis.

Sophie Cabot Black's poems have appeared or are forthcoming in *The Atlantic*, *Agni*, *Field*, *Ploughshares*, and *The Partisan Review*. Most recently she received the 1988 Grolier Poetry Prize and fellowships from the MacDowell Colony and the Fine Arts Work Center in Provincetown.

Marilyn Boe lives in Bloomington, Minnesota. Her poems have appeared in *Passages North*, *The Christian Century*, *Great River Review*, *Iowa Woman*, *Loonfeather*, and other publications.

Jill Breckenridge's book of poems and prose about the Civil War, *Civil Blood*, was published by Milkweed Editions in 1986. "Bottled" and "Unlocking the Doors" are from *How to Be Lucky*, the 1990 winner of the Bluestem Award, Bluestem Press, Emporia State University, Emporia, Kansas. Her poems have been included in many small press publications including *Poetry Now*, *Kansas Quarterly*, *Minnesota Writes: Poetry*, *Dakotah Territory*, and *25 Minnesota Poets*. She has received several fellowships for her work.

Grace Caroline Bridges is a Minneapolis psychotherapist in private practice. Her poems have appeared in *The Evergreen Chronicles*, *The Northland Review*, *Great River Review*, and in the book *JourneyNotes* by Roseann Lloyd and Richard Solly.

Rosario Caicedo was born in Columbia, South America, and has lived in the United States for seventeen years. Her work has appeared in *Sinister Wisdom*, *Sojourner*, *Embers*, *El Taller Literario*, and other publications and anthologies. She lives with her two children in Connecticut and has recently completed work on her first poetry manuscript.

*Kathleen Cain* lived in Tarbert, County Kerry, Ireland, during 1986 and 1987, the village her family came from out of the Great Famine. She is a contributing editor for *The Bloomsbury Review* and lives in Denver.

*Catalina Cariaga* was born on New Year's Day (1958) in Los Angeles to two Filipino immigrants—Augusta and Saturnino. A member of the Kearny Street Workshop (San Francisco), her poems, literary reviews and essays have appeared in *Poetry Flash*, *Tea Leaves*, *Poetry Miscellany*, and *Frogpond*, the Journal of the Haiku Society of America.

*Carlota Caulfield* was born in Havana, Cuba, in 1953. She graduated with a degree in History from the University of Havana and received an M.A. in Spanish from San Francisco State University. She has lived in Zurich, New York, San Francisco and New Orleans. She is currently teaching and finishing her Ph.D. at Tulane University.

*Marilyn Chin* was born in Hong Kong and raised in Portland, Oregon. Her first book of poems, *Dwarf Bamboo*, was nominated for the Bay Area Book Reviewers Award in 1987. She has worked as a translator for the International Writing Program in Iowa City. She has won several awards for her poetry including an NEA fellowship, the Stegner Fellowship at Stanford University and the Mary Roberts Reinhart Award. She is presently teaching in the M.F.A. Program in Creative Writing at San Diego State University.

*Florence Dacey's* work includes *The Swoon*, the libretto for the opera "Lightning," and *The Necklace*, published by Midwest Villages and Voices Press. She lives with her daughter Fay in Cottonwood, a small town in Southwest Minnesota.

*Regina deCormier-Shekerjian* has won the Pablo Neruda Award and the National Jewish Book Award for her work. *Flutes of Bone, Bones of Clay* will be published in 1990 by Mesilla Press. Recent work has appeared in *Salmagundi*, *The Massachusetts Review*, *The American Voice*, *Commonweal*, and *Helicon Nine*, and her book of translations of French poetry for *A Christine de Pisan Reader* is being published by Persea Books.

*Diana Der Hovanessian* was born in the United States and learned Armenian at Harvard. She has translated eight volumes of Armenian poetry including the award-winning *Anthology of Armenian Poetry* from Columbia University Press. Her own work has appeared in *American Scholar*, *The Partisan Review*, and is collected in two volumes, *About Time* and *How To Choose Your Past*.

*Norita Dittberner-Jax* teaches imaginative writing to students of all ages. Her poetry and prose have been widely published. She has moved out of the old Victorian house referred to in this volume and has started a new life.

*Chitra Divakaruni* comes from India and now lives and writes in the San Francisco Bay area, where she also teaches English at Foothill College, and Yoga. Her work has appeared in *The Beloit Poetry Journal*, *Occident*, *Calyx*, *Woman of Power*, *Colorado Review*, and other journals. She has a book of poems, *Dark Like the River*.

*Joan Dobbie* was born in 1946 of Jewish refugee parents in Switzerland. Her family came to America in 1948. She has lived most of her life in northern New York, but has also lived in Boston, Eugene, Oregon, and Puerto Rico. She has two children, writes and teaches poetry, and also teaches Hatha Yoga. She has an M.F.A. in Creative Writing from the University of Oregon. Her poems have been widely published.

*Lorraine Duggin* teaches creative writing and literature at Creighton University in Omaha and is an artist-in-residence with the Nebraska and Iowa Arts Councils. Her poetry and fiction have appeared in *Prairie Schooner, All My Grandmothers Could Sing: Poems by Nebraska Women, North American Review,* and other magazines and anthologies.

*Christine Dumaine* is a doctoral candidate in Creative Writing at the University of Southwestern Louisiana. She has won the American Academy of Poets contest, and the Deep South Writers Contest.

*Rhina Espaillat* is Dominican by birth, the daughter of political exiles, and has lived in New York since the age of seven. She has been writing since early childhood, chiefly in English, and has published poems in a number of magazines and anthologies.

*Marta Fenyves* is a native of Hungary, and author of *From A Distance,* Warthog Press. She makes her home in New Jersey.

*Rina Ferrarelli* is an immigrant from Italy, and came to America at the age of fifteen. She graduated from Carlow College and Duquesne University, and now teaches English part-time at the University of Pittsburgh. She has published her poems in many journals and anthologies including *American Sports Poems,* from Orchard Books, *The Dream Book: An Anthology of Writing by Italian American Women,* from Schocken, *Laurel Review, MSS,* and *Tar River Poetry.* Her first book of translations, *Light Without Motion,* is just out from Owl Creek Press.

*Margot Fortunato* spent summers in her mother's North Dakota hometown. She grew up in South Carolina and now has returned for good to the Midwest where she teaches and publishes poetry and memoir.

*Brigitte Frase* is a writer and critic. She is Contributing Editor of *The Hungry Mind Review* and is co-authoring a book on the avant-garde, tentatively titled *Art By Accident.* She was born in Germany and immigrated to the U.S. with her parents when she was a child.

*Lucia Cordell Getsi* is the author of *Bottleships: For Daughters: Teeth Mother Letters;* and *No One Taught This Filly to Dance* (all poetry volumes); and *Georg Trakl: Poems* (a translation). The recipient of numerous awards and prizes, she is Professor of English and Comparative Literature at Illinois State University. The poem included here is from her new manuscript entitled *Intensive Care.*

――――

Diane Glancy has published two books of poetry: *One Age In A Dream* and *Offering*. A third collection, *The Tonta Poems*, won the Capricorn Prize from *The Writer's Voice* and will be published in the spring of 1990. She is Assistant Professor of English at Macalester College in St. Paul.

judy f. ham's poems have appeared in recent issues of *Rhino, Koroné, The Rectangle, Towers,* and *Ariel*. In the Spring of 1989 she received the Lucien Stryk Award for Poetry.

Carolina Hospital is a Cuban-American writer, residing in Miami where she teaches writing at Miami Dade Community College. Her short fiction, essays and poetry have appeared in *The Americas Review, Linden Lane, Polyphony*, an anthology of Florida poets, *Caribbean Review*, and *Cuban American Writers: Los Atrevidos*, the first anthology of Cuban Americans writing directly in English, which she also edited. She has just completed work on her first collection of poems, *Letters Put Away*.

Pegatha Hughes was raised in Rochester, New York, the daughter of transplanted Iowans, graduated from the State University of Iowa in American Studies, and later taught piano. The mother of two grown sons, she was first published in 1988 in *Minnesota Women's Press* and *Loonfeather*.

Sara Hunter has worked as a medical/technical writer, editor, and a clinical psychologist.

Maureen Hurley is a poet, painter, and photographer who has received several California Arts Council Artist-in-Residency grants and awards. She teaches poetry and visual arts workshops to children and adults. She spends much of her free time traveling in Latin America and was an exchange artist in the Ukraine, Soviet Union, the summer of 1989. Her work has been translated into Spanish and Russian.

Sibyl James is a poet and teacher who sometimes lives in Seattle, Washington. She has taught in the United States, China, and Mexico. She is currently a Fulbright professor at the University of Tunis, Tunisia. Her publications include *The White Junk of Love, Again: Vallarta Street*; and *In China With Harpo and Karl*.

Julia Kasdorf grew up in Pennsylvania and now lives in Brooklyn, a neighbor of immigrants and exiles.

Gayle Kaune's poems have appeared in several literary magazines including *Centennial Review, Greenfield Review*, and the *Seattle Review*. A new chapbook, *Concentric Circles*, has just been published by Hume Press, Chico, California.

Melanie Kaye/Kantrowitz is the author of *My Jewish Face & Other Stories* (Spinsters/Aunt Lute, 1990), and *We Speak in Code: poems and other writing* (Motherroot, 1980), co-editor of *The Tribe of Dina: A Jewish Women's Anthology* (Beacon, 1989), former editor of *Sinister Wisdom*, one of the oldest lesbian/feminist journals in the United States. She supervises independent M.A. students in the Midwest, through the Vermont College Graduate Program, and is active in working for peace between Israel and Palestine.

Patricia Kirkpatrick is a poet who lives in St. Paul, and has completed a manuscript, *Century's Road*.

Irena Klepfisz is an activist in the lesbian and Jewish communities. She is a co-editor of *The Tribe of Dina: A Jewish Women's Anthology* (Beacon Press) and the author of *Keeper of Accounts*. Two volumes of her selected poems and selected speeches and essays will be published by Eighth Mountain Press in 1990.

Charlene Langfur is the author of a book of poems, *Essential Dreams* (1981), and recently published in *Voices For Peace* and *Earth's Daughters*. She holds an M.A. from the Syracuse University Writing Program, and presently teaches writing at William Paterson College in New Jersey.

Jacqueline Lapidus was born in New York City, and lived abroad for twenty-one years, first in Greece, then in France where she became active in the feminist movement. Now based in Provincetown and Boston, she is the author of four books of poems and works at various other forms of wordsmithing.

Joan Larkin is known for the honest and powerful understatement of her poems. Her first book is *Housework*, her second *A Long Sound*.

Barbara Lau of Austin, Texas, has published poems and novel excerpts in various literary magazines and national anthologies, including *Spoon River Quarterly*, *Koroné IV & V*, *The Chiron Review*, *The Tie That Binds*, and *When I Grow Old I Shall Wear Purple*. She has an M.A. in Literature from Sangamon State University, Illinois, and attended the 1988 Iowa Summer Writers' Workshop.

Denise Levertov grew up in England and has lived in the U.S. for many years. She has published 23 books (poems, essays, and translations).

Bea Liu was born in Northfield, Minnesota, graduated from Carleton College, and spent ten years in China as the wife of a Chinese professor. She has published poems and stories, and a book for children, *Little Wu and the Watermelons*, which won the Follett Award in 1954 and the William Allen White Award the following year. She is currently seeking a publisher for a book about civilian life in China during the war with Japan. She lives now in Minneapolis, taking care of her ninety-one year old brother.

Audre Lorde is the author of nine volumes of poetry; her most recent volume *Our Dead Behind Us* was published by Norton in the U.S. and in the U.K. by Sheba Feminist Publishers.

Belkis Cuza Malé was born in Cuba in 1942. Her books of poetry include *El riento en la pared*, 1962, *Tiempos de sol*, 1963, *Cartas a Ana Frank*, 1966, and *Woman On the Front Lines*, Bilingual Edition, 1987. Her biography, *El clarel y la rosa* was published in 1984, and she has completed work on several other volumes of poetry and two novels. She is the founder and editor of *Linden Lane Magazine*, which she publishes in Princeton, New Jersey, with her husband, the Cuban poet, Heberto Padilla.

*Elizabeth Mische John* is a graduate student in the University of Minnesota's Program for Creative and Professional Writing. Her poems have appeared in *Aideron, Passages North, Plainswoman, Christianity and Literature*, and other publications.

*Beverly Acuff Momoi* lives in Minneapolis and writes fiction and poetry. She was a 1989 Loft-McKnight winner in poetry.

*Ilze Mueller* began writing in her late forties. She is from Latvia, teaches languages, and translates poetry and fiction from Latvian and German.

*Lesléa Newman's* books include: *Good Enough To Eat, Love Me Like You Mean It, A Letter To Harvey Milk*, and *Heather Has Two Mommies*. In 1989 she was awarded a Massachusetts Artist Fellowship in Poetry.

*Sharon Olds* has published three volumes of poetry—*Satan Says, The Dead and the Living*, and *The Gold Cell*.

*Cynthia Olson* lives in Minneapolis with her daughter Danielle. Her poems have been published by the *Minnesota Women's Press, Hazelden Press*, and *Harper & Row*.

*Ana Luisa Ortiz de Montellano* was born in Mexico of a Mexican poet father and a British American teacher mother. She writes, "My mixed heritage makes me an exile wherever I live yet gives me a wide range of creative and cultural options."

*Christina Pacosz's* most recent collection of poems is *This Is Not A Place To Sing*, West End, 1987. She is in her final year as North Carolina Visiting Artist at Asheville-Buncombe Technical Community College, Asheville, North Carolina.

*Nancy Paddock* is co-author, with Joe Paddock and Carol Bly, of *Soil and Survival: Land Stewardship and the Future of American Agriculture*, Sierra Club, 1986. Her poems have appeared in many publications including *The Poet Dreaming in the Artist's House, WARM Journal, Sing Heavenly Muse!, Milkweed Chronicle*, and *Feminist Studies*. She is the author of *A Dark Light*, Vanilla Press.

*Nancy Peterson* writes that her creative work includes playing with two daughters, Meghan Aisha and Hannah Jamila, with special education pre-school children, and with words, and time with her husband, Chester.

*Sandra Price* writes feature articles for visual arts magazines in a converted boiler house in St. Paul, Minnesota, and on a float house in the Queen Charlotte Islands.

*Sheila Richter* lives in south Minneapolis with her daughters Hannah and Merry and their dog, Benchley. She writes, "I've always had 'strange' thoughts, but only recently began writing them down."

*Pattiann Rogers* is the author of four volumes of poems, most recently *Splitting and Binding* from Wesleyan in 1989. She is the recipient of a Guggenheim Fellowship and two NEA Grants. She was the Richard Hugo Poet-in-Residence at the University of Montana in 1987.

Lois Roma-Deeley has published work in various literary magazines, most recently in Iris: A Journal For Women, and Oxford. She works at Arizona State University.

Helen Ruggieri's article on Alice Corbin Henderson, an early poet, will appear in Belles Lettres in 1990. She writes, "The poem, "Forked Tongue" is for an ancestor, Scottish writer Lewis Grassie Gibbon, who had some unique ideas about language which I used in the poem."

Maureen Seaton has poems in Iowa Review, Massachusetts Review, Poetry Northwest, New Letters; and poems forthcoming in Chelsea, Ploughshares, and Southwest Review, among others. She has two daughters and is currently involved in the healing arts in New York City.

Gail Shafarman is a poet, mother, ocean watcher, therapist, bird lover, and fellow human being on this beautiful and troubled planet. She has had poems published in many small magazines including Heaven Bone, The Literary Review, and Edge Wing Press.

Mary Crescenzo Simons is an interdisciplinary artist whose recent poetry installation, "Native American," has appeared in the United States through Objets Vend'art. She is currently working on a biography of Chief Mankiller.

Sophie Slingeland was born in Zurich, Switzerland, and grew up in a Swiss-Eastern European family. Her family spoke Russian, French, German and Polish. She writes, "My first language was Russian; I started learning Swiss German and German when I started school, then English and French from the seventh grade on, and I learned to speak Dutch when I met my husband."

Lusia Slomkowska's professions are writing and produce farming. She is completing her first book of poetry, entitled The Polka Hour. Her lesbian sports-romance, Softball Summer, is forthcoming from Rising Tide Press. She is translating the work of the Polish poet, Teresa Ferenc, and has also recently planted three hundred crowns of asparagus.

Dona Luongo Stein's work has appeared in Colorado Review, Denver Quarterly, EPOCH, and Greenfield Review, Ploughshares, and Sojourner, among others, and in anthologies and in the collection Children of the Mafiosi, West End Press. A former Stegner Fellow in Poetry at Stanford University, she is now working on a collection of poems about women in opera called Heroines of the Opera. She edits poetry for Matrix.

Julia Stein is a poet, fiction writer, and reviewer, and has published a volume of poetry, Under the Ladder to Heaven.

Lori Storie-Pahlitzsch developed the Writers' Workshop at the Greenville, South Carolina Fine Arts Center, where she was Writer-in-Residence for four years. She has been named to the South Carolina Reader's Circuit for 1989–1990. Her work has appeared in Poetry Northwest, The Crescent Review, and in other journals.

*Meredith Stricker*, daughter of a World War II refugee, grew up in California with the opaque and untranslated sounds of her mother's language—Hungarian—as paradigm for any voice threatened by extinction. She has worked in performance collaborations, received an M.F.A. from the Iowa Writer's Workshop, and currently is co-editor of *HOW(ever* Magazine. Her work has appeared recently in *EPOCH, Ink*, and her translations of poet Zsuzsa Takacs' work appear in the *New Hungarian Quarterly*.

*Stephanie Strickland* is using her National Endowment for the Arts Award to complete a book of poems about Simone Weil. Her chapbook, *Beyond This Silence*, is published by State Street Press.

*Cinda Thompson* is a native of the Midwest. She has received several awards for both poetry and short fiction and has published in both literary magazines and anthologies. She believes most in "keeping it simple."

*Dina Uahupirapi* grew up in her home in Namibia. She is currently studying economics at Hamline University in St. Paul, Minnesota.

*Barbara Unger* has published four books of poetry. *Learning To Foxtrot*, her most recent collection, appeared in 1989. A fiction collection, *Dhing For Uncle Ray and Other Stories*, is due to be published in 1990. Recently poems of hers have been published or accepted for publication by *Denver Quarterly, South Coast Review*, and *North Dakota Quarterly*.

*Gloria Vando's* poems have appeared in numerous magazines including *New Letters, Rambike, Stiletto, Windfall*, and in forthcoming anthologies *Kansas City Out Loud II, Back In My Body*, and *The Denny Poems*. She was awarded the 1989 Kansas Arts Commission Fellowship in Poetry, and has been a poet-in-the-schools for the Missouri Arts Council. She is the founding editor of *Helicon Nine*.

*Marisella Veiga* was born in Havana, Cuba. In 1960 her family went into exile. She was raised both in St. Paul, Minnesota and in Miami, Florida, where she currently lives. She received a B.A. in English from Macalester College, and an M.F.A. in Creative Writing from Bowling Green State University. Her poetry has appeared in several literary magazines. While living in Puerto Rico, she worked as a freelance business writer as well as an international news reporter. A former artist-in-residence at Altos de Chavon, in the Dominican Republic, she is currently an English language editor and translator for an international publication.

*Alice Walker* is widely acclaimed for her poems, essays, and novels.

*Teresa Whitman* is a graduate student at the University of Minnesota where she won The Academy of American Poets Award in 1988. She lives with her two children in St. Paul.

*Mitsuye Yamada* is the author of *Desert Run: Poems and Stories*, from Kitchen Table Press. Work of hers also appeared in *This Bridge Called My Back*. She has retired from teaching at Cypress College in California.

————

Deborah Keenan is a poet, the author of *The Only Window That Counts* and *Household Wounds* (New Rivers Press), *One Angel Then* (Midnight Paper Sales), and co-author of *How We Missed Belgium* (Milkweed Editions). She is a recipient of a Bush Foundation Artist Fellowship and a National Endowment for the Arts Fellowship in Poetry.

Roseann Lloyd's latest book is *JourneyNotes*, a collaboration with writer Richard Solly (Harper/Hazelden). Her collection of poems, *Tap Dancing For Big Mom*, is published by New Rivers Press. She is also the co-translator, from the Norwegian, of *The House with the Blind Glass Windows* (Seal Press). She is currently at work on a new collection of poems.

# Index of Authors

## Looking for Home

was designed by Jodee C. Kulp
in Monotype Joanna type
and printed on 60 lb natural stock
by Edwards Brothers of Ann Arbor, Michigan.
The cover photograph is by
Ruth Thorne-Thomsen.
Art direction by R.W. Scholes